WYRE FOREST RECIPES

BY
CATHERINE ROTHWELL

Illustrations By
Eilen Kershaw & Chris Redman

OTHER BOOKS BY THE AUTHOR

BOOKS AVAILABLE

PRINTWISE PUBLICATIONS LTD.
41 Willan Estate, Vere Street, (off Eccles New Road), Salford, M5 2GR.
Ports of the North West
Bright and Breezy Blackpool

RICHARD NETHERWOOD LTD.
Fulstone Barn, New Mill, Huddersfield, HD7 7DL.
Old Devon Recipes
Old Somerset Recipes
Old Hertfordshire Recipes

HENDON PUBLISHING CO. LTD.
Hendon Mill, Nelson, Lancashire, BB9 8AD.
Old Cornwall Recipes
Old Kent Recipes
Old Sussex Recipes

EUROPEAN LIBRARY
Post Office Box 49, 5300 A. A. , Zaltbommel, Netherlands.
Fleetwood in Old Picture Postcards Vol. 2
Bournemouth in Old Picture Postcards

WYRE FOREST
RECIPES

Published in 1992 by
COMMA INTERNATIONAL
Biological Systems
Lower Coed Morgan,
Abergavenny, Gwent, U. K.
(0873) 840256

British Library Cataloguing in Publication Data

A catalogue record for this book is
available from the British Library

ISBN 0 9513977 3 7

Designed & produced by Images Design & Print Ltd, Hanley Swan
Printed & bound in Great Britain by Billing & Sons, Worcester

CONTENTS

ABOUT THE AUTHOR

Born in the Prestwich area of Manchester, Catherine Rothwell has resided in the Fylde Coast of Lancashire for the past thirty years. During her career she was Deputy Borough Librarian of Fleetwood and, after reorganisation, was placed in charge of all Local History and Reference for the Lancashire District of Wyre.

Her writing career has been prolific. For her thesis on HISTORY OF FLEETWOOD-ON-WYRE she was awarded a Fellowship of the Library Association, and this work formed the basis of her first pictorial history of Fleetwood, FLEETWOOD AS IT WAS. The success of this and its companion book THE FYLDE AS IT WAS reviewed as "a classic of its kind", led to further commissions. To date thirty-nine titles have been published, of which twenty-eight are local history books covering different areas of Lancashire and as far afield as the Isle of Man, Isle of Wight, Bournemouth and Torquay. The other eleven titles are Regional Recipe books on Lancashire, Cornwall, Kent, Sussex and the Midlands.

Catherine Rothwell has been a frequent contributer to such magazines as *Lancashire Life, The Lady, Lake Scene* and *Preview of Lakeland*. She has appeared on B.B.C. and Granada Television, B.B.C. Radio Lancashire, Manchester, Coventry and Warwick, Isle of Man and Red Rose Radio, and has lectured for the W.E.A. and to Local Associations and Groups.

LANCASHIRE SEA STORIES

"as comprehensive and well-written a compilation of maritime episodes as one's ever likely to find . . . Thoroughly recommended."
Lancashire Life

LANCASHIRE: PHOTOGRAPHIC TOUCHSTONES OF A BYGONE AGE

"Altogether a collection inspiring the best of all recommendations: it leaves you wishing for more."
Lancashire Life

GARSTANG IN TIMES PAST

"It is the spirit of the ordinary folk which shines from the pages of this book."
Garstang Courier

WYRESDALE IN TIMES PAST

"A brilliant collection of words and pictures."
Lancashire Evening Post

SOUTHPORT IN FOCUS

"A great new publication for your historical bookshelves."
Southport Visitor

FLEETWOOD IN OLD PICTURE POSTCARDS

"Bathe in nostalgia with this delightful collection."
Fleetwood Chronicle
"More than just a picture book: it is in effect a history of Fleetwood and district."
Lancashire Life

PORTS OF THE NORTH WEST

"Maritime history comes alive"
West Lancashire Evening Gazette

AN ALBUM OF THORNTON-CLEVELEYS

" . . . a must for anyone interested in local history."
West Lancashire Evening Gazette

LYTHAM, FRECKLETON AND WREA GREEN IN TIMES PAST

"A hundred years of history in Fylde's villages have been brought back to life."
Lytham St. Anne's Express

ACKNOWLEDGEMENTS

Mr E. Belcher, Bayton
Bewdley Museum
Dr Bones, Harvington
British Broadcasting Corporation
Stanley Butterworth, Bispham
Collectors' Corner, Mirfield
Mrs Cowdray, Rock
Miss Doolittle, Kidderminster
Mr and Mrs R. Ecclestone, Button Oak
Derek Fearnley, Stourport
Mrs N. Gatehouse, Pound Green
Mr and Mrs Edwin George, Button Oak
Mary Hardiman-Jones, Devon
Esther Hendy, Kidderminster
Tom Holland, Mamble
Sheila Houghton, Stourport
Dorothy Lambden, Bayton
Rector Colin Levey, Wilden
The Moat House Restaurant, Harvington
The Postcard Shop, Bewdley
Michael Pulsford, Bewdley
Richard III Society, Harvington
Rev. Dr E.J. Rothwell, Halesowen
Val Ruston, Harvington Hall
Annie Saunders, Kidderminster
Severn Valley Railway
Ron Severs, Preston
Marguerite Stokes, Stourport
Anne Tolley, Kidderminster
Valentia Arms, Arley
Margaret Vaughan, Frome
Nik Walton, Arley
Mr and Mrs R. Williams, Wolverhampton
Woodhouse Farm, Hawkbatch Wood
Wyre Forest District Council

And especially Mrs Kate Howells of Harvington Hall, Chaddesley Corbett and Mr John F. Daniels, Head Chef of The Elms, Abberley. Renowned in their profession, they were generous with their time and gracious with their help, which I greatly appreciate.

Introduction

Almost 28 years ago when my mother came to live in the district of Wyre Forest our frequent and occasionally long visits to Worcestershire commenced, so you could say that Wyre Forest is my second home. Mother brought to the area her considerable skills as housewife and cook, particularly enjoying the plentiful supply of vegetables and fruit. Indeed, she settled so well she never wanted to go back to her native Lancashire and it was here at the wonderful age of 98 that she died just three years ago. This small book is something of a tribute to her for she taught me almost everything I know about cooking.

I can see her now with her bright eyes and thick, wavy hair, stirring lemon cheese (she never called it curd), preparing beetroots or mincemeat, rolling pastry, cutting bread or slicing jaffa oranges all to that miraculous degree of thinness I have never managed to achieve, basting golden chicken and succulent ham smothered in a crowd of baked potatoes or, most exciting, stuffing Christmas goose. In the background of my earliest memories is a large, black, open fire-range. Aloft hung bunches of thyme, sage and rosemary. Oatcakes, slung like washing on a rack near the ceiling, dried out in the fierce heat of the fire, and father's home-brewed beer in a large, brown, earthenware "mug" was placed near the warm hearth-stone to get the yeast working.

It was a proud day when mum made the school Christmas cake and twenty years later my wedding cake, a large portion of the top deck of which we enjoyed on our honeymoon. I have eaten mother's rich fruit cake toiling over Honister Pass in a snowstorm, at Land's End in the boiling sun, on the Clee Hills looking for blackberries in Autumn and in Trafalgar Square by the stone lions with a posse of pigeons waiting for crumbs – a cake for all seasons!

Putting the book together was a mingling of pleasure and pain for there were so many memories: her stay at The Elms, Abberley; her visits to the village schools in primrose time; early snowdrops at Wribbenhall; the jewel-bright Pre-Raphaelite windows at Wilden; Hartlebury Castle; Harvington Hall; trips to Kidderminster and Bewdley. In her going days she loved to talk about all these and was knowledgeable on a number of subjects, including the political career of Stanley Baldwin. Of birds and wild creatures she had a fund of information which she passed on to her children and grandchildren. The year before mother died was the last time the martins flew up from the river to nest at Hill Top. They never came again.

To the end she has been my guardian angel, for although many kind people contributed recipes, others, through modesty, inadequacy or pressure of work, did not. Appropriately amongst these pages are a few of mother's dishes. Although she ate sparingly herself and in the last months of her life nothing at all, she was very much aware of the importance of food, having reared not only her own family through hard times but a dozen little brothers and sisters. Nourishment went hand in hand with nurture.

Talking to older residents of Wyre Forest, I am reminded of her remarkable qualities; her kindness, her sense of humour, her love of high, clean-washed Worcestershire skies, the shining frame of star-spangled heavens as cold Winter approached and especially that swooning mistiness of Summer. One Mother's Day at Hill Top we talked about games, old customs and remedies and my sister Sheila wrote it down. Some of these I have included and my wish is that in these recipes something of her sweetness and goodness may come through.

CATHERINE ROTHWELL

10

Ethel Houghton was born 100 years ago on 8th October 1888. When this photograph was taken she was Ethel Fielden, (before her marriage).

11

Oven Temperature Chart

°C	°F	Gas No.	Description
110	225	¼	Very Slow
120/130	250	½	Very Slow
140	275	1	Slow
150	300	2	Slow
160/170	325	3	Moderate
180	350	4	Moderate
190	375	5	Moderately hot
200	400	6	Moderately hot
220	425	7	Hot
230	450	8	Hot
240	475	9	Very hot

IMPERIAL – METRIC CONVERSION

Quantities are given in Imperial and metric measures. Since exact conversion does not always give convenient quantities for cooking purposes these have been rounded into units as recommended by B.B.C. Books. Never mix Imperial and metric measures in one recipe. Stick to one system or the other.

Where "cups" are referred to:-

1 cup flour = 4oz – 100g
1 cup sugar = 6oz – 175g
1 cup butter = 8oz – 225g

Wyre Forest Hints From Almost 100 Years Ago

- To prevent musty smell in a teapot which is to be packed away, place 2 lumps of sugar inside.

- The smell of fish or onions may be removed from the hands or utensils by rubbing with dry mustard.

- To clean gilt picture frames take a gill (150ml) of malt vinegar in a pint (600ml) of cold water, a large, soft shaving brush and a soft, clean cloth. Remove all dust and brush with solution, doing a small area at a time.

- Drawers that are stubborn slide easily when a wax candle is rubbed on their runners.

- Never wash your face immediately before going into the sun. Rub it well with a slice of cucumber dipped into cream and allow to dry.

- Mirrors should be rubbed daily with a sheet of white tissue paper.

- A recipe for hair restorer: 50ml (2oz) eau de cologne, 1g (½ dram) rosemary, 175ml (6oz) bay rhum. Mix well and apply to roots of hair with a soft sponge.

- If the hands are stiff after a day's washing or scrubbing, take a teaspoon of fine salt and rub them all over with it whilst wet.

- A good way to freshen leather goods is to rub in well the white of an egg with a piece of soft rag. It will give a nice gloss without cracking the leather. A solution of sugar and water brushed over a straw hat stiffens it.

- An economical way of using up candle ends is in starting wood fires. Orange peel dried out in the fire oven makes good kindling.

- Use buttermilk for a sunburned complexion.

- To relieve a bruise take 1 handful of chamomile flowers or elderflowers, 300ml (½ pint) vinegar, 150ml (¼ pint) brandy. Boil flowers in 600ml (1 pint) of water. Strain into jug containing the vinegar and brandy. Apply as hot as comfortable.

- A good wash for the face is 50g (2oz) Pearl Barley to 1.75l (3 pints) water. Boil this until reduced to 1.2l (1 quart) Strain into a bowl then add a spoon of brandy, the juice of 1 lemon and a few drops of camphor oil.

In selecting a fowl for roasting, choose one having dark legs as it is sure to be juicy. Pluck, singe and firmly truss it. It is undoubtedly best roasted before an open fire with incessant basting for 1 hour.

Recommended cooking time for:

a pigeon	:	20-40 mins
a hare	:	1½-2 hours
a rabbit	:	¾-1 hour

It would appear that paraffin was a great standby as a cleaner and that country living was cheaper by use of herbs, root vegetables grown on the family plot, nuts and fruits of the forest, hedgerow dandelions and young nettles for making drinks and herb medicines, cowslip wine, elderberry wine. Bilberries could be picked in season and a careless rapture of summer fruits from the cottage garden: raspberries, gooseberries, black and redcurrants, strawberries was the basis with butter sponge of "Summer Pudding", remembered by so many as a delightful sweet. Country people got up early to gather mushrooms in "known" spots. Windfall apples were free; wild pears, strawberries and cherries were stewed. Swedes and turnips were sometimes free from the farmers, and there was plenty of mint, chives and parsley to pep up the sauces and the stewpot. A jug of "beastings" was enjoyed, a rich, junket-like custard, when a cow had calved. Bacons and hams were hung in cottage kitchens, the longer the better, until they "turned green", which explains references to pieces of green pork in hoggan, a very old recipe for a workman's pasty or lunch, demanding a lusty appetite and a strong stomach.

The deep fire grate with its five bars was kept going all day and alongside the range, a boiler fitted with a tap was heated by the fire. There was a big hook fixed above the fire for the kettle or iron cooking pot. Griddle cooking was available from red embers; cough mixtures (lemon, honey, glycerine, liquorice water) were warmed on the oven shelf to give greater efficacy. Cut onions removed odours from the sick room. A cure for chilblains was to plunge the feet alternately into a bucket of fresh snow and a bucket of hot water. I met an old lady who assured me it had worked for her!

Beef tea, cowheel and beef, jellied eels, were considered strengthening dishes for ailing children, and amongst "nice dishes" for 1897 it was recommended: "Put a kidney inside a large onion and bake in a well buttered dish."

Fried salmon roe: Boil the hard roe of salmon, cod or pike, drain, cool, cover with egg and saute in pan, Serve with chives and parsley.

There was enormous demand that year for Lipton's tea, "Tea Merchants to Her Majesty the Queen". Over one million packets were sold weekly at 5p (1 shilling) to 8p (1 shilling & 7 pence) per pound. On July 23rd 1897 it was announced: "Lipton has paid in duty for this week's clearance of tea the largest cheque ever received by H.M. Customs, London, £35,365.46p (£35,365-9s-2d)." Their fame was such that a letter from abroad addressed simply "Thomas Lipton, England" arrived without delay.

---◆---

Eddie Belcher who has lived all his life in Wyre Forest is shown in his beautiful garden with the ancient tower of Bayton Church behind. Next door to this cottage in which he was born is the now disused smithy. In Bayton Church is a 12th Century font and a very interesting board lettered "Bread to the Poor at St Thomas's Day" c.1827. There was also a bequest for flannel. Eddie remembers people walking miles to get a loaf; he also recalls the funeral of a village lady of 102, the last time the ancient wheel bier was used to bear a coffin. In those days funeral feasts followed the burial.

17

Meat, Game and Fish

Meat, Game and Fish

Our first attempt to meet Edwin George, forester, was unsuccessful as he had "gone off on squirrel control"; so, after collecting recipes from Mrs George at Fallow Lodge, we made for Callow Hill Centre, passing private woodlands from where the cuckoo called repeatedly after the rain shower. Heart-of-the-forest feeling was all around at Furnace Mill, Dingle Spout Coppice, Pump Cottage, Shakenhurst, Far Forest, Dowles Bridge. Dowles Brook, bisecting the Forest of Wyre with its 6,000 acres of oak, beech and birch, certainly has its share of wild life: foxes, otters, badgers, but we saw rabbits, grey squirrels, a kingfisher and a heron. As we walked from Tanglewood, before our eyes a fallow deer suddenly stepped from the dark of the forest into the sunshine, a lovely sight. Near ancient Coach Road to Arley is one of many amazing trees in the Forest, the Seckley beech with 32 trunks.

◆

21

Mr Gillam, basket maker of Button Oak, is shown early this century at his ancient craft. Another forest craft was the making of besoms, used to sweep lawns, gravel drives and stables. The Gillam brothers made all kinds of baskets in all sizes, for animal feeds, clothes, fruit etc. Alf Birch, Jack Brown and Jim Morris were similar craftsmen but we found only one left, making mainly rustic garden furniture.

AN OLD RECIPE FOR TENDERISING AN OLD BIRD AND GETTING THE BEST FLAVOUR FROM IT.

large chicken

2 chopped baby leeks

salt and pepper

300ml (½ pint) dry white wine

2 tablespoons corn oil

4 medium sized sliced onions

2 chopped green apples

seasoned flour

450g (1lb) potatoes

Clean bird, reserving giblets. Remove lumps of chicken fat. Sprinkle with seasoning. Cover the giblets with cold water, season, and bring to boil for ¾ hour. Chop the chicken liver finely and mix with all the stuffing ingredients:

100g (4oz) sausage meat

1 tablespoon breadcrumbs

1 teaspoon thyme

2 chopped cooking apples

1 tablespoon fresh chopped

parsley

Stuff the bird with this

Brown the chicken in heated oil and put into large dish. Add chopped onions, leeks and apples. Season, then pour over the giblet stock and the wine. Cook in a moderate oven, 180°C for 1½ hours.

The potatoes should be peeled, sliced, rolled in seasoned flour and added to the casserole about one hour before finish of cooking time.

HOW TO COOK AN OLD DUCK

1 duck 1.5kg-1.75kg (3½-4lb weight)

salt and pepper   2 tablespoons sherry

50g (2oz) butter   25g (1oz) seasoned flour

450g (1lb) freshly shelled peas   600ml (1 pint) stock

1 tablespoon chopped fresh mint

1 egg yolk beaten in 1 tablespoon of thin cream

1 teaspoon chopped fresh herbs

Brown the cleaned duck, dusted all over with seasoned flour, in the heated butter. Pour off fat and add sherry, stock and herbs. Season to taste and simmer for an hour. Add the peas and cook on for another hour at a steady simmer. The beaten egg and cream are stirred in at the end and not allowed to boil. This sauce is served with the duck and peas, the tablespoon of freshly chopped mint scattered over.

Old-fashioned carving terms come to mind in dealing with poultry and game, some Victorians excelling at the florid expression: spoiling a hen; winging a partridge; embracing a mallard; thighing a woodcock. The 18th century accompaniments to meat dishes were know as tracklements and might consist of melon and orange/peaches, redcurrants or wild raspberry stuffing. Today's universally accepted extra for duck seems to be orange sauce, but real fruit jellies containing scant sweetening e.g. redcurrant, rowan or rose hip jelly are excellent, cutting any fattiness that may be present.

VENISON WITH SAUCE

Rub the joint of venison well with lard, cover with foil and roast at 180°C 35 minutes to the pound. Allow to brown, towards the end, by removing foil.

300ml (½ pint) red wine
1 tablespoon flour
3 teaspoons mashed anchovy
1 teaspoon thyme
1 onion

Collect the juices from the roast venison and add the chopped onion. Stir in flour, wine, anchovy and thyme. Cook, stirring all the time until it thickens. Serve with the venison.

Venison was served hundreds of years ago in halls and Mediaeval castles when those "below the salt", i.e. the peasantry, were served "umbles", the entrails of deer, and so ate humble pie. Those above the salt received the choice roast venison.

—————————————◆—————————————

ROAST PARTRIDGE IN SHERRY SAUCE

2 roasted partridges	100g (4oz) lean chopped ham
50g (2oz) butter	50g (2oz) mushrooms
1 small onion finely chopped	1 small carrot finely chopped
bay leaf	200ml (⅓ pint) sherry
25g (1oz) flour	600ml (1 pint) chicken stock
1 level tablespoon chopped parsley	½ teaspoon thyme

Divide the cooked partridges into joints. Heat butter in a large pan, add mushrooms, carrot, onion, bay leaf, parsley, thyme and ham. Gently fry then sprinkle with flour. Stir in stock and sherry and simmer until liquid is reduced by ⅓. Add the partridge pieces, gently cook on for about 10 minutes. Serve hot with a watercress and tomato side salad.

Roger and Anna Eccleston of Tanglewood Guest House, Button Oak, Bewdley, describe two of their recipes, Pork and Parsley and Rhubarb Sponge Pudding, as "very simple, but incredibly popular with all ages". We sampled them and agree heartily. After a day in the Forest they complement each other perfectly. Rhubarb Sponge Pudding you will find with "Bread, Cakes, Puddings".

◆

PORK AND PARSLEY (serves 4 – 5)

700g (1½lb) boned pork, well trimmed and diced (not too small)
1 large onion
1 tablespoon oil
100g (4oz) piece of gammon (smoked)
300ml (½ pint) stock (chicken or vegetable)
150ml (¼ pint) white wine (or all stock if preferred)
450g (1lb) potatoes
black pepper
Plenty of chopped parsley

Brown the meat in 2 batches to seal. Add the onion and diced gammon. Stir round for a few minutes. Add stock (and wine if preferred) pepper. Stir some more. Cover. Cook gently for 45 minutes until meat is tender. Peel potatoes, cut into even-sized pieces and add to the pan. Bring slowly to just below the boil, then reduce heat and simmer till potatoes are just tender. Add the parsley. (Sometimes I thicken the gravy a little.)

Good with peas and carrots or cabbage and thyme.

PIGEON PIE

Pluck, singe and draw pigeons. Wash well under cold running water. Roast or boil for 30 minutes. When slightly cooled, remove flesh and place in a pie dish with juices and a sprinkle of herbs. Either line a greased dish with pastry or put on a pie lid. Cook for a further 20 minutes in hot oven till pastry has browned.

Flaky pastry (see recipe) is very nice for pigeon pie, which I print as given to me. In the testing, I felt that boiling was a surer way of dealing with the birds and that a pie lid of flaky pastry cooked at 200°C for the given time worked best.

With his wife Lucy whom he married in 1892, Stanley Baldwin and Lord
Stanley are campaigning in 1929 for the National Government. A great lover of
Worcestershire, to which he escaped from the pressures of parliament, he was
Conservative Member for Bewdley 1908-1937 and is best remembered for his
handling of the crisis leading to the abdication of Edward VIII after only 325
days' reign.

FLAKY PASTRY

225g (8oz) flour   175g (6oz) margarine

1 level teaspoon salt   cold water

Sieve the flour and salt, taking ¼ of the margarine to rub into the flour. Roll into a rectangle. Take another ¼ of the margarine and spread it in knobs over the pastry. Fold in 3, seal edges, roll and repeat this process until all the margarine is worked into the pastry. Use light, quick movements and have everything cold.

♦

THE FORESTER'S WAY WITH VENISON

This is based on an 18th century recipe. Made into venison pasty it must have been as convenient to take into the forest as the Cornish pasty was to take down the mine.

1kg (2lb) shoulder or breast of
venison cut up
bunch of herbs
salt and pepper
225g (8oz) flaky pastry

50g (2oz) butter
50g (2oz) seasoned flour
juice of 1 lemon
600ml (1 pint) stock
a little red wine and beaten egg

The meat should be well covered with the seasoned flour. Melt butter in a pan and fry meat until brown on all sides. Add lemon juice, herbs, seasoning and sufficient stock and red wine to cover the meat. After bringing to the boil, simmer gently for 1½ hours or until meat is tender. Place in a large pie dish and cover. Roll out the flaky pastry if you want to make pasties in rounds like a dinner plate. Place portions of venison with its juices down the centre, fold over other half of pasty, crimping outer edges together after moistening with cold water. Brush on the glaze of beaten egg, which turns a golden brown in the oven. Place pasties on a baking sheet and cook at 180°C for 30 minutes.

◆

ANNE SAUNDERS' CASSEROLE OF RABBIT OR VENISON

Joint either the rabbit or venison. This method does for either. Then, in the casserole make 1. a layer of rabbit or venison, 2. a layer of fresh breadcrumbs, 3. a layer of thinly sliced onion rings, 4. a good sprinkle of rubbed sage.

Half fill the casserole with water. Add "a nut of fat", a sprinkle of pepper and salt, and for 2½ hours cook the covered casserole in the oven at 180°C Rough cuts of venison will take longer in the cooking. Ensure that you have enough moisture in the pot. Some people like to add gravy browning at the end to provide colour.

◆

JUGGED HARE - *from Woodhouse Farm*

1 large hare, jointed   1 dessertspoon herbes de Provence
50g (2oz) butter   50g (2oz) wholemeal flour
grated nutmeg   6 grinds of peppercorn mill
600ml (1 pint) cider   1 onion

Cut hare into small pieces and season each piece. Brown the meat in butter and place in an earthenware pot or jug with sliced onion and the herbes de Provence. Pour in cider and seal well. Put pot into water jacket, at least ⅔ up the jug. After boiling point is reached, simmer slowly for 3 hours, topping up the water to keep it well up the vessel containing the hare. Stir flour into melted butter in a pan, adding some of juices from hare. Stir till gravy thickens and flour has cooked then pour back over the hare and serve.

The farmer's wife, who used to be a Miss Doolittle, was one of the busiest and most knowledgeable ladies on the subject of Wyre Forest that we met. We could have talked to her for hours. In her version of Jugged Hare she sometimes adds pureed tomatoes for a change.

◆

SAGE

SEVERN BROWN TROUT

3 cleaned trout, traditionally with head and tail left on
sea salt and freshly ground pepper
150ml (¼ pint) cider
good squeeze of lemon
1 teaspoon chopped parsley in a cup of diluted tarragon vinegar

Pat trout dry and place in a dish, tailed and headed if required. The ovenproof dish should then receive the seasoning, cider, lemon juice and herbs in vinegar. Cover and bake for 25 minutes at 180°C Baste, then place "nuts" of butter all over the fish and replace in oven without lid to brown thoroughly, about another 7 minutes. In the 18th century river trout was also made into pies.

◆

The Bailiff's House, Bewdley, built by Thomas Bolston in 1610, is a beautiful example of timber-framing for which Worcestershire and neighbouring counties became well known. The Manor House across from the Redthorne was built about the same time, both reflecting Bewdley's prosperous river trade.

FISH PIE

"Using boiled fish of any kind, some stock for white sauce, 25g (1oz) butter, 25g (1oz) flour, red ground peppers. Mix all together (25g (1oz) parsley if liked added to it). Place in well buttered oven proof dish. Cover with boiled mashed potatoes to which has been added 75g (3oz) grated cheese and ½ teaspoon mustard. Bake in oven for about 20 minutes. Serve with peas."

COD POTATO

1kg (2lb) conger eel – cod can be used instead

Boil in salted water until tender. Have ready some boiled potatoes with skins on. Serve together with thin or double cream. Just pour on from the container, adding pepper and salt to taste.

"This is a fish dish we were fond of."

OR

"Another fish dish was boiled cod mixed with equal amounts of boiled potato, chopped parsley, egg for mixing, salt and pepper. Roll into small flat cakes then in seasoned flour and fry until brown on both sides. Any kind of fish can be used."

STEWED EELS

1.5kg (3lb) skinned eels cut up	4 tablespoons oil
20 button mushrooms	600ml (1 pint) red wine
175g (6oz) chopped, skinned onions	seasoned flour
freshly ground sea salt and black pepper	lemon slices
1 tablespoon soft butter	1 tablespoon flour

Toss eel in flour, seasoned with salt and pepper. Heat oil in a stew pan and brown the eel pieces. Remove eel and saute onion. Put back the eel slices, add mushrooms, wine and seasoning and simmer for 30 minutes or until tender. Knead butter and flour together and thicken the eel liquor with this by adding small pieces gradually, stirring all the time. You will feel the sauce thicken smoothly. Serve with the lemon slices as garnish.

EEL PIE

2 good sized eels or elvers of about same weight, stewed with mushrooms, parsley, onion, 2 glasses of sherry, 1 glass of Worcester sauce and lemon juice. Put in a pie dish, top with slices of hard-boiled egg and cover with pastry. Cook for 30 minutes at 200°C.

In 12 acres of formal gardens, the Elms, built by architect Gilbert White, a pupil of Sir Christopher Wren, is now a Country House Hotel of international reputation, one of the top 300 hotels of the world.

Head Chef, John F. Daniels, contributes the following Welcome Wyre Forest Recipes.

WILD SALMON GLAZED WITH A CHIVE SABAYON

one portion

50g (2oz) prepared salmon very thinly sliced	1 yolk of egg
25g (1oz) diced eating apple	25g (1oz) shallot
25g 50ml (2 fl.oz) fish stock	(1oz) diced cucumber
25ml (1 fl.oz) double cream "A"	
1 tablespoon whipped double cream "B"	
good pinch chives, finely chopped	
50ml (2 fl.oz) dry white wine	lemon juice

Place apple and cucumber in centre of a 25.5cm (10 inch) plate. Arrange sliced salmon on top; season with a little salt. In a small pan reduce the chopped shallot, fish stock, white wine and a few drops of lemon juice till syrupy. Add double cream "A" and reduce by half. Cool slightly and add egg yolk and whipped double cream "B". Season to taste. Strain sauce, mix in chives and pour over salmon. Place under salamander and grill for 2-3 minutes, when sauce should have good glaze.

◆

CHIVES

Soups and Savouries

This photograph from 1897 shows John Lowe and Brothers' Rope Works, founded at Wribbenhall in 1801 on the east bank of the River Severn. They also manufactured twine, using a hand-cranked twisting jack for shroud laid rope (the central strand around which the others were twisted). The hacker's job was to dress or "hackle" the fibres before they were spun.

43

Joined by my sister, a resident of Stourport-on-Severn, we spent a most productive day walking the town, including a tour of the busy canal basin, talking to many people. Sloping lawns from the Tontine with its classic lines, five doorways and carved stone acanthus leaves, led to rows of moored narrow boats, amidst them Snipe, Taurus and Jupiter, now cruising hotels each for 11 passengers under the direction of chef-trained Derek Fearnley whose own favourite dish is lobster with garlic butter. The Maid of Steel was being re-tarred; Krisandi made her way through 3 locks to the river. With history all around from the single-span iron bridge, lock shop with old canal keeper's cottage below, bell, Angel, Anchor, Severn Trow, to V.R. posting box, Parkes Passage and York Street with its row of Georgian buildings, we literally improved the shining hour, for all was bathed in golden sunshine, by talking Food.

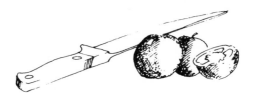

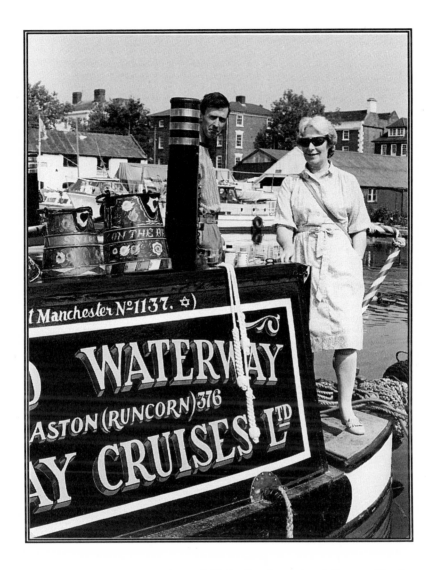

Proprietor/Chef Derek Fearnley and Sheila Houghton aboard Taurus. We all admired the authentic touches from the days of the canal narrow boats: ribbon plates and hand-painted pails. Typical cruises are Stourport – Stratford, Stourport – Nantwich, Chester – Llangollen, and a typical dinner menu: Cucumber Mousse, Lamb Chops with Shrewsbury Sauce, Baked Trout stuffed with Mushrooms, Lemon Chicken with Fennel Salad, Syllabub and Sherry Trifle.

KATE HOWELL'S PARSNIP SOUP

50g (2oz) butter

3 large onions

600ml (1 pint) milk

freshly ground salt and pepper

2 teaspoons curry powder

1kg (2lb) parsnips

1.2l (2 pints) chicken stock

Melt the butter and add chopped onions and curry powder. Cook for 5 minutes then add the cleaned, roughly chopped parsnips. After 5 minutes add stock and seasoning. Cook until parsnips are tender. Liquidise and return to pan. Add milk and taste to check seasoning. Serve garnished with red apple, diced and tossed in lemon juice.

This is one of the best-flavoured soups we have ever tasted in our wanderings around 5 regions.

◆

TOMATO SOUP

450g (1lb) ripe tomatoes

1 bay leaf

600ml (1 pint) chicken stock

grated lemon rind

seasoning

1 small onion

1 clove of garlic, crushed.

lemon juice

a little cream

Cut up tomatoes and put in pan. Add stock and heat. Add chopped onion, bay leaf, lemon rind, garlic and seasoning. Bring to boil and simmer for one hour. Sieve and add lemon juice. Add cream when ready to serve with grated lemon rind on top.

LENTIL SOUP FROM BEWDLEY

450g (1lb) red lentils, washed and soaked

1½ large onions   3 crushed cloves of garlic

2 tablespoons oil   600ml (1 pint) chicken stock

1 teaspoon ground cumin   ½ teaspoon ground sea salt

juice of 1 small lemon

Fry onions in oil in a large pan till brown. Stir in garlic. Put in lentils and stock and boil. Stir in cumin. Do not add salt till lentils are softening. Add water if necessary. Stir in lemon juice and serve with a teaspoon of chopped chives or parsley in centre of bowl.

GARLIC

OLD-FASHIONED BROTH

Rub 1.5kg (3lb) brisket beef daily with salt for 3-4 days. Put in a saucepan with chopped carrots, chopped onion, diced turnip and chopped leek if available. For the last 20 minutes add chopped curly green cabbage. The broth is eaten first, then the beef and boiled potatoes. Any beef left over is delicious when cold. Cooking time takes two hours' simmering.

◆

KIDDLEY OR KETTLE BROTH

"Peel and cut up 3 onions. Simmer for about an hour with a thick rasher of bacon salted lightly. Add pepper and 25-50g (1-2oz) dripping. Sieve the broth, pour over squares of stale bread and eat very hot, say on a cold night."

◆

TRIPE AND ONIONS

Wash tripe and cut into small pieces about 5cm   (2 inches) long. Put into frying pan with plenty of sliced onions. Add seasoned milk and fry over gentle heat until tender. Serve with boiled potatoes.

◆

HAWNE TAVERN MEAT BALLS

450g (1lb) minced steak   1 well chopped onion
½ teaspoon ground cinnamon

Work all ingredients together, adding a little wholemeal flour to roll the balls in and shape them. These small meat balls can be dropped into soup and simmered for at least half an hour. 15 minutes before serving, 3 tablespoons of cooked rice could also be added to the soup for further nourishment. With crusty rolls this makes a family meal, followed by fruit.

◆

POTATO THATCHED MEAT LOAF

2 slices bread 1cm (½ inch) thick   150ml (¼ pint) milk
1.5kg (3lb) minced beef   2 sticks celery chopped
2 tablespoons mango chutney   2 rashers bacon diced
1 beef stock cube made up   1 level teaspoon salt
1.5kg (3lb) creamed potatoes

Soak the bread in milk for ½ hour. Mix all ingredients except creamed potatoes, using two 1kg (2lb) loaf tins. Place a slice of soaked bread in the bottom of each tin and divide the mixture between the two. Bake in moderate oven for one hour. Drain off any fat and turn onto serving dish. Cover with mashed potato, marking it with a fork. Brown in oven for a further ½ to ¾ hour. For most purposes half quantities will suffice.

CHICK PEA DIP

Tahina is the oily paste from crushed sesame seeds. It has been used in making hummus in the Middle East for centuries and because of today's widespread travel has become popular in Britain, travelling to Wyre Forest.

175g (6oz) chick peas soaked well beforehand
4 tablespoons tahina   4 crushed cloves of garlic
juice of 1 lemon   ground sea salt
2 tablespoons olive oil

Drain and boil chick peas in fresh water for 1 hour. Put in blender with small measure of their cooking water to make into a paste. Add tahina, lemon juice, olive oil and garlic. Blend. Add ground sea salt to taste. It should be the consistency of thin cream. If desired, ½ teaspoon of cumin can also be added.

51

CHICKEN IN SHERRY SAUCE

Another excellent recipe from the Moatside Restaurant at
Harvington Hall.

1 roast chicken, meat removed from bones	25g (1oz) flour
300ml (½ pint) chicken stock	25g (1oz) butter
50g (2oz) Cheddar cheese	300ml (½ pint) milk
2 teaspoons Dijon mustard	salt and pepper
1 tablespoon dry sherry	a little Tarragon

Melt butter and add flour. Slowly add stock and cook until
thickened. Add all other ingredients except chicken and bring
to a simmer. Pour half of the sauce into an ovenware dish, add
chicken pieces, followed by the rest of the sauce. Top with a
cup of breadcrumbs and a knob of butter. Cook in oven at 170°C
until it bubbles, but do not allow to dry out.

◆

ARLEY SCRAMBLED EGG

Nic Walton, Manager and Chef of the Valentia Arms, who was
trained at the Dorchester Hotel, Park Lane, serves river trout,
peppered venison, Dover sole, pork fillets, king prawns, wood
pigeon, local game in cranberry and port, Paris mushrooms,
quail breasts in salad, and salmon tartare i.e. wild salmon
marinaded in gin and white wine, an impressive, ever-
changing with the seasons, gallimaufrey of fare. I thought his
scrambled egg at breakfast the lightest, most delicately-
flavoured ever. He told me that fines herbes bring out the egg
flavour best of all, but very light poaching in a mould must be
part of the answer. Perhaps two eggs whisked with a nut of
butter, a little thin cream, seasoning and fines herbes? Nic
wasn't saying, but I tried it out and the result was good. I used a
bare ½ teaspoon of the herbes.

DROVERS' PIE

From Kidderminster

Drovers' Pie, convenient protein "on the hoof", was a favourite of field workers and the drovers who travelled long distances herding cattle to the market towns.

I was told that traditionally the filling goes into a very thin pastry case in the form of a pie or pasty. It consists of lean minced lamb finely chopped, half an onion, black peppercorn, seasoning and a sprig of rosemary. This is topped with mashed potato. Cook for half an hour on high temperature 200°C. The meat filling is best pre-cooked with a good nut of butter and a little water, well sealed in a lidded casserole, for about ¾ hour on the same temperature. Keep moist, and if made into a pasty, seal in as Venison Pasty.

◆

MAMBLE LAMB PIPKIN

"In a fireproof pipkin place cubed neck end of lamb or mutton with fat removed, add 2 chopped courgettes, a small handful of sultanas, a tablespoon of washed rice, 100g (¼lb) shelled peas. Cook in cider or wine. On the top place a thick layer of sliced potatoes as in hot pot."

These are directions from a busy chef. The lamb keeps very hot in this traditional cooking pot, and the wine and sultanas make it rather special. Cooking time is about 1¾ hours on 190°C. A little basting of the potato topping with butter makes them brown, or you can simply shake the pipkin gently ½ hour before cooking time finishes. The juices over-running the potatoes brown them nicely.

CHICKEN LIVERS

100g (4oz) chicken livers

75g (3oz) softened butter

freshly ground black pepper

sea salt

½ teaspoon dried sage

4 tablespoons brandy

Wash livers, removing skin. Heat 25g (1oz) butter and gently cook the livers for not more than 4 minutes. Pound the livers in a mortar or liquidise, then add to them 25g (1oz) butter, the brandy, seasoning and sage. Mix all well together and pot in small earthenware containers. Melt the remaining butter and pour over to seal. Cover with foil and refrigerate. The potted chicken liver is good spread thickly on wholemeal open sandwiches. We followed this with a bunch of sweet seedless grapes.

◆

STOURPORT POTATO CAKES

2 generous cups mashed potato

25g (1oz) melted butter

4 heaped tablespoons S.R. flour

2 tablespoons brown sugar

pinch of ginger or cinnamon

150ml (¼ pint) milk

Mix together all the dry ingredients then add melted butter and finally mix to a stiff paste with milk. Place on a floured board and knead. Roll to 2.5cm (1 inch) thickness and cut into rounds. Bake on both sides on a medium griddle or in hot oven 200°C for 20 minutes. Serve hot with butter straight away.

SANDWICH SUGGESTIONS FROM WYRE FOREST

- Wensleydale cheese chopped with apple and celery.

- Hazelnut pate spread

- "Decker" sandwiches: beef burger, thin crisp bacon, wafer thin omelette spread with mustard.

- Garlic butter spread: cream 1 cup of butter with 3 cloves crushed garlic.

- Anchovy butter: cream 1 cup butter, beat in 4 minced anchovy fillets.

- Curry butter: cream 1 cup butter and beat in ½ teaspoon curry powder with 6 grinds peppercorn.

- Parsley butter: cream 1 cup butter and beat in ½ cup minced parsley and chives and 2 tablespoons lemon juice.

- ¼ sliced banana with ½ chopped eating apple, lemon juice squeezed over. Spread on wholemeal bread thick with honey butter.

- "A nice piece of roast ham cut thin, followed by some good broth" – (a lady at Sayers Alms Houses).

A Severn Valley train in the 1960s, after following the trackbed of the old line to Cleobury, Tenbury and Woofferton, turns and heads westward into Wyre Forest, the line crossing the Severn at Dowles Bridge. Early crews on the footplate enjoyed fry-ups on a clean fireman's shovel: bacon, sausage, tomatoes and white bread sizzled in 4oz lard for 2 minutes over a glowing fire-box and they were done to a turn.

BREAD. CAKES.
PUDDINGS. PIES.

The Old Bakery at Hartlebury, like that at Arley, may well have once been the site of a communal oven for the village. It certainly conjured up the scent of yeast, sacks of wholemeal flour and bread and cake baking.

Grandmothers and great grandmothers who once lived in or near Wyre Forest used to bake once a week, storing up to 20 loaves in large, wooden boxes. Pork pies and cakes would also be baked and it was the men's job to cut wood from the forest for firing the oven.

Many old Wyre Foresters recall the days of keeping a pig, basis for food all the year round. Black puddings, brawn, sausages, chitterlings, trotters, and bacon, the latter cured in the smoke of slow-burning oak sawdust from the forest, were all on the menu. It was sometimes the village constable's task to despatch piggy, but some villages had an itinerant pigsticker who wore a floppy hat and wide, black, leather belt in which he stuck the tools of his trade. Some great grandmothers could do the whole job themselves provided there was lots of boiling water and a pig table. When a pig was killed the whole village benefitted for a single family could not use all the trimmings.

WHOLEMEAL COTTAGE LOAVES

1.5kg (3lb) stoneground wholewheat flour

25g (1oz) dried yeast   25g (1oz) lard

1 tablespoon salt   1 tablespoon brown sugar

1 crushed vitamin C tablet   1l (1¾ pints) warm water

Crush the vitamin C tablet amongst the sugar and place ⅓ of the warm water into a bowl. Into this whisk the dried yeast and leave in a warm place.

In a large mixing bowl place flour, salt and lard. Rub the fat into the flour, stir in the yeast mixture and mix all thoroughly with the flat of the hand

Turn the dough onto a floured surface and knead it well to work the yeast throughout. After 10 minutes' kneading divide the dough into 2 large pieces and 2 smaller. Making traditional cottage loaves, place one above the other, the top half the size of the base. Make a hole in the top which penetrates to the second layer. Cover loosely with greased polythene or a clean tea towel and leave to rise for 30 minutes. Bake at 230°C in a pre-heated oven for 35 minutes. This makes 2 cottage loaves. Bread that is correctly baked sounds hollow when the base of the loaf is tapped by the knuckles. The addition of vitamin C to an old recipe obviates the need for lengthy proving by strengthening the gluten.

◆

MRS GEORGE'S SCONES

225g (½lb) S.R. flour

75g (3oz) soft margarine

50g (2 oz) currants

A good pinch of allspice

1 teaspoon baking powder

25g (1oz) sugar

milk to mix

Rub the margarine into the flour and baking powder until the mixture looks like breadcrumbs. Add the rest of the ingredients with sufficient milk to make a soft dough. Roll out on a floured board and cut into individual scones, using a cutter or floured top of a wine glass. Flour the top of each scone and bake at 200°C for 15-20 minutes until nicely browned and risen.

◆

BUTTON OAK SULTANA SCONES

225g (8oz) wholemeal flour

50g (2oz) soft margarine or butter

150ml (¼ pint) milk

¼ teaspoon cinnamon

75g (3oz) sultanas

2 teaspoons baking powder

Grease a baking tray and set oven at 200°C. Sift flour, baking powder and cinnamon into the bowl and rub in the margarine or butter until the mixture looks like fine breadcrumbs. Mix in the sultanas and bind with the milk to form a dough. Roll this out on a floured surface and cut rounds. Transfer to trays, glazing the scones with a little milk or beaten egg and bake for 15 minutes in centre of oven which must be the right temperature to ensure scones with soft inside and crusty outside. Use them fresh.

ETHEL'S RICH FRUIT CAKE

275g (10oz) plain flour mixed with tsp. baking powder

225g (8oz) butter   225g (8oz) brown sugar

4 free range eggs   25g (1oz) glace cherries

750g (1½lb) mixed dried fruit   25g (1oz) ground almonds

1 level teaspoon mixed spice   25g (1oz) chopped candied peel

Line and grease an 18cm (7 inch) square or 20.5cm (8 inch) round cake tin and surround with double brown paper. Set oven at 150°C. Prepare cake by the creaming method. Sift in flour and spice. Stir in the cleaned fruit, ground almonds and a little milk if necessary to bring about a dropping consistency. Turn into the prepared tin and smooth the top. Make a slight hollow centrally to allow for rising. Bake 3-3½ hours. 1st hour 150°C, 2nd hour 140°C, 3rd hour 120°C.

◆

RASPBERRY PAVLOVA

3 egg whites   ½ teaspoon vanilla essence

175g (6oz) caster sugar   1 teaspoon white vinegar

2 level teaspoons cornflour   300ml (½ pint) double cream

350g (12oz) fresh raspberries sprinkled with sugar

Set oven at 120°C place an oiled sheet of greaseproof paper on a baking sheet. Beat egg whites till very stiff and beat in half of sugar. Mix cornflour with rest of sugar and fold this gently into egg mixture. Fold in the vanilla essence and vinegar. Pile meringue mixture in a round shape onto greaseproof paper on a baking sheet. Bake for 1 hour until risen and light brown. Leave to cool then remove from paper. Whip the cream, pile on to the pavlova then pile on raspberries.

This photograph from 1912 shows the Town Hall, Kidderminster, with the statue of Rowland Hill, father of the Penny Post, in the foreground. The old days at Kidderminster are still spoken of with longing: "It was like one big happy family in the carpet works." John Brinton had the oldest carpet-weaving firm, the latter replacing weaving when that declined.

63

HARTLEBURY EASTER CAKES

175g (6oz) plain flour   100g (4oz) butter

Rub fat lightly into sieved flour, press together and roll out to 0.5cm (¼ inch) thickness. Cut into rounds and place on greaseproof paper on a baking sheet. Cover each cake with caster sugar the same thickness as the cake. Allow to stand overnight then bake 20 minutes at 300°C Cakes should be pale and not brown in colour. Handle carefully so as not to lose the sugar, stacking in a tin with layers of greaseproof paper between each.

◆

LEMON CAKE

100g (4oz) caster sugar   100g (4oz) butter

2 eggs   100g (4oz) flour

½ level teaspoon baking powder   grated rind of lemon

Cream butter and sugar. Beat in eggs, flour, lemon rind and lastly baking powder. Bake in middle of oven at 190°C. Use lemon flavoured butter cream filling and lemon icing for the top of the cake. Orange sponge can be made by substituting orange for lemon.

MINCE PIE PASTRY

150g (5oz) flour   100g (4oz) margarine

1 egg yolk   1 teaspoon rum

1 tablespoon cream

Rub margarine into flour until it resembles breadcrumbs. Make a well in the centre and add egg yolk, rum and cream. Mix all together until a pliable dough is formed. Place in the fridge for 10 minutes then roll out pastry thinly.

Cut into small rounds and line greased patty tins. Fill with mincemeat and place rounds on tops to form lids. Brush with beaten egg and bake in a hot oven 200°C until golden brown.

◆

TRADITIONAL GINGERBREAD

sold at fairs

175g (6oz) black treacle   150ml (¼ pint) milk

1 level teaspoon bicarbonate of soda   100g (4oz) margarine

1 level teaspoon cream of tartar   350g (12oz) plain flour

50g (2oz) chopped peel   175g (6oz) demerara sugar

1 good dessertspoon ground ginger

Warm the milk and treacle together. Sift flour with ginger, bicarbonate of soda and cream of tartar. Rub in margarine until it looks like fine breadcrumbs. Mix in sugar and peel. Stir in milk and treacle and mix well. Pour mixture into well-greased tin and bake for 1½ hours at 150°C. Halved almonds and slices of crystallised ginger can be scattered on top half way through cooking time, but these are one up on tradition.

FOREST GREEN POUND CAKE

450g (1lb) butter   450g (1lb) sugar

450g (1lb) flour   8 eggs

1 wine glass brandy   grated rind of large orange

(50g (2oz) candied peel,

225g (8oz) sultanas and almonds could be added)

This is an early Victorian Wyre Forest farmhouse recipe made by the creaming method. The farms seem to have passed on amounts and methods by word of mouth from one generation to another. Beat all well together. Use a large cake tin and cook for about 1½ hours at 180°C.

◆

KIDDERMINSTER FIG FLAPJACK

This flapjack emerges from the oven about 5cm   (2 inches) thick with its bottom layer of crumble, thick layer of mashed figs and dates, topped by more crumble, which is simply made.

225g (8oz) oats   100g (4oz) butter

100g (4oz) demerara sugar

Cream butter and sugar then stir in oats. Press firmly into tin and bake at 150°C following directions above. The fig mixture consists of equal quantities of stewed figs and packet dates mashed together with a little golden syrup and a teaspoon of warm water. Cooking time is about 30 minutes.

CALLOW HILL NUT CAKE

This recipe is very similar to one I was given in Kitzbuhel, Austria, and I suspect it flourished originally in forested areas with a good supply of hazel nuts in Autumn. There they called it Esterhazyschnitte and use almonds when cobnuts are not available.

white of 4 eggs   225g (8oz) sugar
225g (8oz) rubbed almonds or hazel nuts

Whisk the egg white till it is stiff, then add the sugar and rubbed almonds. Place in a buttered baking tin and cook in a moderate oven for about 30 minutes. Immediately after baking, cut the cake in broad slices. Stuff the slices with chopped glace cherries and cream and glaze with a white glazing.

(The reference to "rubbed" almonds in this recipe means finely chopped and blanched.)

◆

HAZEL NUTS

RHUBARB SPONGE PUDDING

450g (1lb) rhubarb

100g (4oz) butter

2 eggs

ginger

4 tablespoons golden syrup

100g (4oz) sugar

100g (4oz) S.R. flour

Cut up the rhubarb in a well-buttered pie dish. Trickle the syrup over it. Cream the butter and sugar. Add the eggs, one at a time, beating in well. Then fold in the flour and some dry ginger to taste and spread over the fruit. Bake for 40 minutes or so at 190°C, gas mark 5, until golden brown.

◆

QUEEN VICTORIA'S SHORTBREAD

350g (¾lb) flour

100g (¼lb) sugar

225g (½lb) butter

Rub in the butter and sugar on a board, then work in the flour with finger tips. The dough should then be rolled out 0.25cm (¹/₈th inch) thick, cut into circles and pricked with a fork. Bake on a greased tray in a moderate oven for 15 minutes.

As an alternative to Bayton Raspberry Jam, the fruit pulp from Raspberry Gin could be used with these shortbreads.

The Queen was very fond of these and they became popular in many regions.

CHRISTMAS PUDDING

100g (4oz) sultanas

100g (4oz) currants

100g (4oz) raisins

50g (2oz) peel

50g (2oz) chopped almonds

100g (4oz) plain flour

100g (4oz) brown breadcrumbs

1 small carrot finely grated

100g (4oz) grated suet

1 apple cored and grated

¼ level teaspoon ground cinnamon

75ml (3fl.oz) sherry

½ level teaspoon mixed spice

3 eggs

100g (4oz) demerara sugar

3 tablespoons brandy

grated rind and juice of 1 small lemon

Put the ingredients in a bowl in the order listed and mix well.
Put mixture in two 450g (1lb) bowls and steam for 8 hours.

*Woodhouse Farm of 150 acres includes Hawkbatch Wood, part of Wyre Forest.
This fine, yeoman farmer's house, typical of the area, is about 300 years old,
built upon stone, but parts go back to the 14th Century. In the 1920s many of
these farms stood empty. Today Woodhouse rears sheep and cattle, has a Swiss
Simmental bull for breeding, grows beet crops and potatoes, and does contract
work using a precision drill for sowing beet.*

71

STEAK AND KIDNEY PUDDING

The pastry is made from:

225g (8oz) S.R. Flour   75g (3oz) shredded suet
Sufficient cold water to make a smooth, not sticky dough.

Pudding filling:

450g (1lb) lean braising steak   100g (4oz) kidney
1 onion peeled and chopped   300ml (½ pint) marmite stock
2 tablespoons seasoned flour

Wash steak and kidney, coring the latter and cutting the steak into small squares. Toss all these pieces in the seasoned flour. It is quick and handy to pressure cook the meat, as to steam it raw in the pastry takes at least three hours. In the pressure cooker allow 20 minutes. Roll out pastry and line the pudding basin, cutting a circular piece for pudding lid. Put the cooked meat into this basin and fill ¾ full with gravy. Press the lid firmly to the moistened edges of the pudding and cover with foil allowing for the pudding to rise in cooking. Pressure cooked it will take a preliminary 15 minutes plus 45 minutes at 2.25kg (5lb) pressure. Put at least 900ml (1½ pints) water in the pressure cooker and stand pudding basin on trivet.

———————————————◆———————————————

BEEF AND MUSHROOM PIE

225g (8oz) lean minced beef

1 large onion

seasoning

100g (4oz) mushrooms

50g (2oz) margarine

Cook the minced beef then add mushrooms and seasoning. Slice and chop onion finely. Place minced beef and mushrooms in a greased pie dish and cover with the onions. A pastry lid for the pie can be made from rubbing 100g (4oz) lard into 225g (8oz) flour. Bind with a little water and roll out in a circle to fit the pie dish, dampening the outer edges. Make pastry leaves from the trimmings and glaze with egg yolk. Bake at 200°C for ½ hour.

◆

CHEESE AND CHUTNEY PIE

225g (8oz) short crust pastry

25g (1oz) flour

175g (6oz) grated Cheddar cheese

3 tablespoons chutney

2 eggs

25g (1oz) butter

300ml (½ pint) milk

Line a 20.5cm (8-inch) tin with pastry. Make a roux with the butter, flour and milk. Add seasoning and egg yolks. Stirring well, cook for 5 minutes. Add grated cheese. Continue stirring. Beat egg whites until stiff. Spread chutney in bottom of pie. Fold stiff egg whites into the cheese sauce and pour onto chutney. Top with pastry and brush with beaten egg. Bake in hot oven 218°C for ½ hour.

SAUSAGE SPLITS

450g (1lb) pork sausage

450g (1lb) cooked mashed potato

1 dessertspoon tomato ketchup

sprinkle of garlic salt

pepper

Grill sausages. Drain and place on kitchen paper. Cut down centre of each sausage but not right through. Open out. Add to mashed potato the garlic salt, ketchup and pepper. Pipe potato mixture down centre of each open sausage. Place under grill and serve hot with water cress or accompanied with Carrot and Apple Salad, which you will find amongst "Salads and Drinks".

PORK MEAT LOAF

450g (1lb) minced raw pork	225g (½lb) minced raw beef
2 rashers minced raw bacon	1 medium onion grated
6 tablespoons white breadcrumbs	2 tablespoons milk
1 teaspoon herbes de Provence	1 egg beaten well
1 tablespoon milk	1 tablespoon water

Put meats, onion, fresh breadcrumbs, egg, herbs, milk and water all together in a mixing bowl. Put in seasoning (black pepper and sea salt freshly milled) and stir thoroughly. Form this mixture into a roll about 20.5cm (8 inches) long, wrap in greaseproof paper and finally secure it well with foil. Place the meat roll in a tin with about 5cm (2 inches) of hot water in the bottom and bake in centre of a moderate oven for 2 hours. On the top shelf of the oven place 4 scrubbed potatoes marked with a cross. These can accompany the meat loaf whose ideal other companion consists of hot button sprouts. Any meat loaf left over will slice up admirably cold. Do not try to reheat it.

Glazed broccoli also makes a good accompaniment to many meat dishes:

2 medium broccoli spears	1 small onion
150ml (¼ pint) vegetable stock	1 celery heart

Cut the stems off the broccoli about 5cm (2 inches) below the flowers. Slice the onion and celery. Put vegetables in a saucepan with the stock. Bring to boil then lower to simmering rate. Cook for 20 minutes until broccoli and celery are tender, adding a little extra stock which eventually reduces to a syrup.

PORK PIE

Hot Water Crust

225g (8oz) plain flour   75g (3oz) lard
150ml (¼ pint)milk and water

Place milk and water in a pan with the lard and melt. Sieve
the flour into a bowl, making a well in the centre. Pour liquid
from pan into well and mix, kneading a little until smooth. Cut
⅓ of pastry for lid and keep it warm. Roll one piece for bottom
and one for sides.

Filling

350g (¾lb) minced pork   scattering of mixed herbs
½ teaspoon salt   dash of cayenne pepper
2 tablespoons stock   ½ level teaspoon gelatine

Place pork, herbs, seasoning in a bowl and mix well. Put into
pie. Put lid on and pinch pastry well together round the top.
Make a small hole in the middle of the lid and decorate with
pastry leaves. Brush over with egg yolk and bake in a hot oven
218°C for one hour, reducing to 180°C for ½ hour. Melt gelatine in
stock and pour into pie slowly through hole in lid.

◆

Oak Bark from Wyre Forest was widely used in the Bewdley tanyards. Hundreds of years ago half the bark money was given to the King and the other half to the Bark Bailiff, but in this century Oakes and Todd, timber hauliers, sold the forest bark to agents for the tanyards.

The bark peelers, as shown in this photograph from 1900, were mainly women but a bark-peeling team might include whole families who travelled daily to the forest from their cottages, some by pony and trap. The flat, cloth caps or straw hats of the women in the photograph enabled them to carry home loads of faggots on their heads.

It was a seasonal occupation linked to the coppicing system. In Wyre, April 24th to June 14th was traditionally considered the best time for bark peeling, when the sap was rising in the branches. Innumberable oak shoots sprang from the roots of trees and were cut down every year. The bark was stripped, the remaining "black poles" being sold to make fencing and hurdles. It was customary amongst the teams to "bark the shins" of any newcomer but to avoid this painful experience, "treating" the rest of the party was usually the best answer. On June 13th Bewdley's great fair for the sale of cattle, horses, and cheese was held, an occasion on which to spend the money earned. Beacalls, the last of Bewdley's tanyards, closed in 1928.

VEAL, HAM AND EGG PIE

Using same hot water crust pastry and same method:

225g (½lb) minced veal
100g (¼lb) minced streaky bacon
1 teaspoon chopped fresh parsley
pinch of mixed herbs
1 hard-boiled egg
dash of sea salt and pepper

Mix ingredients, layering with the sliced, hard-boiled egg. Place in pie and bake as before, also adding stock slowly with gelatine through hole in pie crust as before.

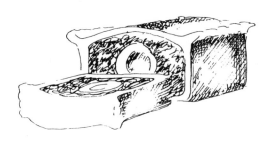

◆

SAVOURY MEAT PIE

Pastry

225g (8oz) flour   100g (4oz) lard

a little water

Filling

35g (1½oz) butter   1 onion

3 tomatoes (skinned)   75g (3oz) mushrooms

225g (½lb) cooked minced beef   15g (½ oz) flour

Prepare the pastry by rubbing fat into flour until it resembles
breadcrumbs. Form into dough by adding a little water. Line a
swiss roll tin with the pastry, leaving sufficient to make a
latticed top. Melt the butter and saute chopped onion,
mushrooms and tomatoes. Cook slowly together, adding the
flour and a little seasoning. Stir well into the minced beef.
Place this filling into pastry case and using a latticed
formation with strips of pastry, cover the top. Bake in a hot
oven 220°C for ½ hour. Garnish with tomatoes and parsley.

◆

CHICKEN AND MUSHROOM PIES

225g (8oz) short crust pastry prepared as in previous recipe.
Roll out and line patty tins.

Filling

15g (½oz) flour	15g (½oz) butter
150ml (¼ pint) milk	175g (6oz) chopped chicken
50g (2oz) chopped mushrooms	a little finely chopped parsley

Make a sauce by blending the flour, milk and chopped parsley.
Saute the chopped mushrooms in the butter. Into each patty tin
place a portion of chicken, mushrooms and sauce, then cover
with pastry lids. Bake in hot oven for 25 minutes.

◆

APPLE AND RAISIN PIE

1 kg (2lb) cooking apples	75g (3oz) raisins
100g (4oz) soft brown sugar	275g (10oz) S.R. flour
75g (3oz) lard	50g (2oz) margarine
2 tablespoons cornflour	

Rub the fat into the flour to make the pastry. Roll out half and
line a 25.5cm (10-inch) pie plate. Do not stretch the pastry.
Peel, core and slice apples. Put apples in a pan of boiling water
with the raisins for only 2 minutes. Drain well. Put half the
fruit into pie base. Mix together the cornflour and brown sugar.
Put remaining apple and raisins over this and the rest of the
sugar mixture. Roll out pie crust and put in position on top,
wetting edges of pastry. Make a hole in top of crust, glaze with
milk and scatter on a little sugar. Bake in centre of oven at
200°C for 15 minutes then reduce heat to 170°C for 30 minutes.

Members of the Richard III Society at Harvington Hall practising archery. The Society is interested in studying the life and times of Richard III and annually visits the battlefield at Bosworth around August 22nd. They also enjoy a banquet in the splendid mediæval surroundings of the great house at Harvington.

81

AUNT PHYLLIS'S MINCEMEAT

225g (½lb) currants

225g (½lb) Demerara sugar

225g (½lb) shredded beef suet

100g (4oz) grated apple

4 tablespoons brandy

finely grated juice and rind of 1 lemon

225g (½lb) raisins

50g (2oz) candied peel

1 teaspoon allspice

½ nutmeg grated

1 teaspoon cinnamon

The raisins etc., if it is necessary to wash them, should be thoroughly dried before use. Mother "improved" on this recipe by adding 25g (1oz) of chopped nuts to every 450g (1lb) of mincemeat. Mix all the ingredients together. Stir well and ask anyone around to do likewise and make a wish as they stir.

Unfortunately, we missed "All You Want To Know About Herbs" by Mrs Kim Hurst at Hartlebury Castle. However, we arrived at Harvington Hall on one of the best days of the year, May 21st, and were delighted to meet members of the Richard III Society. Talking to Val Ruston in the kitchen, we heard about the use of herbs in mediaeval cookery: fennel, lovage, borage, mint, rosemary, saffron for colouring, and the lavish use of honey, for no sugar was then available.

In Upper Arley was the home of Sir Robert de Burgh who in the reign of King John persuaded the King to sign Magna Carta giving more power to the barons. The photograph from the 1930s shows that part of the River Severn that could once be crossed by chain ferry aided by the swift current.

In those days cooked peacocks brought to the long refectory table in the Great Hall would be displayed in their beautiful feathers. Porpoise and beaver, regarded as fish, could be eaten on Wednesdays and Fridays to make a change. Highly prized marchpanes and dried fruits figured at the banquets with florentines and sweet pies, but first came eggs in broth, turbot broth, baked venison, fresh salmon, herrings, beef, rabbit, roast kid or moor fowl. For purely academic interest I include this ancient recipe from Harvington.

EGG PIE

Take the yolks of 24 eggs; in those days eggs were much smaller.

225g (½lb) fresh butter

Beat all well and strain to eliminate "cock threads". Add 3 teaspoons of rose water, 1 mace blade and a little honey. Then "harden paste in ye oven."

Amidst the tangy wood smoke an appetising Beef Stew was in the making on the open range. I was told it contained lentils, oats, beef, chopped cabbage, leek, swede, carrots and parsnips, cooking together with a bunch of mixed fresh herbs in the pot.

Surrounded by small "butts" for storing wines, cheese moulds, oak dough trough, ladles, massive hooks and cooking pots, the atmosphere was just right, whilst outside the sun blazed down and archers in mediaeval costume, watched by long-robed ladies, shot arrows at the target.

SALADS and DRINKS.

CARROT AND APPLE SALAD

4 tablespoons grated raw carrot

2 teaspoons lemon juice

4 tablespoons chopped apple

1 tablespoon thin cream

1 tablespoon seedless raisins

water cress or lettuce for base

Put lemon juice and cream in a bowl and mix to make a dressing. Blend carrot, raisins and apple and toss in the dressing. Pile onto green base.

$$\blacklozenge$$

WILDEN ORANGE SALAD

3 teaspoons ground cinnamon

6 oranges

2 tablespoons orange flower water

Peel or with sharp knife remove all pith. Cut into thin slices across the orange. Arrange. Sprinkle with the flower water and spread lightly the cinnamon all over.

$$\blacklozenge$$

DRIED FRUIT SALAD

225g (8oz) dried apricots
50g (2oz) sultanas
50g (2oz) sliced blanched almonds
75g (3oz) prunes
1 teaspoon orange flower water

Leave all ingredients to macerate for 2 days in enough water to cover them. This is important for flavour. There is no need to cook, but if wanted immediately, simmer all for 25 minutes, adding flower water at the end. To thicken the juice, add extra apricots which have been soaked previously. These can be put in a blender and added as puree to the confection.

Country women favoured these in winter when fresh fruit was not available and as an alternative to syrup of figs medicine.

◆

An old gas lamp and quaint enamelled signs transport the passenger back to the days of the Great Western Railway. The flourishing Severn Valley Railway now runs between Bridgnorth and Kidderminster. Steam engines haul preserved carriages past stations like this where time seems to have stood still. Many of the trains have catering facilities whilst hot meals and real ales are available at Bridgnorth, Bewdley and Kidderminster.

SPICY SALAD

For use with curries

2 tablespoons raisins

sea salt and freshly ground pepper

100g (4oz) salted peanuts

½ bunch washed, chopped Spring onions

2 tablespoons lemon juice

1 small red or green pepper, seeded, chopped and washed

4 tablespoons mayonnaise

2 bananas

Peel and slice bananas, put in bowl and sprinkle with lemon juice. Add chopped pepper, onions, raisins, mayonnaise, salt and pepper. Stir in the peanuts and serve immediately.

◆

DORA'S COLESLAW

350g (12oz) white cabbage	1 small onion
3 tablespoons mayonnaise	50g (2oz) sultanas
2 medium carrots	
freshly ground black pepper and sea salt	

Wash and shred cabbage, scrape and grate carrots, peel and chop finely the onion. Put all in a bowl with the sultanas, mayonnaise etc. and mix well. This should be well covered and left at bottom of fridge for at least 2 hours before serving.

MAYONNAISE

2 egg yolks

1 teaspoon dry mustard

300ml (10 fl.oz) sunflower oil

3 teaspoons white vinegar

1 teaspoon salt

12 turns of pepper mill

3 teaspoons lemon juice

By hand or in a blender. If by hand, put egg yolks into a small bowl with salt, mustard and pepper. Whisk in the oil, one drop at a time. When the mixture thickens nicely you can pour in the rest of the oil. Add lemon juice and vinegar.

◆

VINAIGRETTE DRESSING

½ teaspoon sea salt ground fine

freshly ground black pepper

2 tablespoons wine vinegar

6 tablespoons olive oil

Shake all ingredients in a screw top jar. Chopped chives or 1 teaspoon dry mustard can be added.

◆

'SHERRY'

1.5kg (3lb) stoned raisins   1.5kg (3lb) soft brown sugar
3 medium potatoes grated   handful pearl barley
25g (1oz) yeast

Boil 4.5l (8 pints) of water and pour onto barley. When cooled a little, add all other ingredients except yeast. When lukewarm, sprinkle yeast on top. Leave for 4 weeks, stirring every day. Strain and then filter liquid into dark bottles.

◆

MOTHER'S LEMON SQUASH

6 lemons   1.5kg (3lb) sugar
25g (1oz) citric acid   1.2l (2 pints) boiling water

Wash lemons, grate rind into jug, squeeze juice and put in all remainder of lemons as well. Add citric acid, sugar and boiling water. Stir well, strain and add water to taste. This squash is lovely, ice cold, for a sore throat.

◆

WHET CUP

This was a drink before dinner to whet the appetite, a Victorian recipe for iced punch, again with brief, terse directions.

600ml (1 pint) fruit syrup

600ml (1 pint) pineapple juice

300ml (½ pint) Jamaica rum

300ml (½ pint) weak tea

1 bottle champagne

orange zest

cinnamon sprinkle

Mix all. Chill. I have not tested this expensive recipe, but I am saving up.

◆

FOREST MEAD

9l (2 gallons) soft water

2 egg whites

40g (1½oz) yeast

2.25 kg (5lb) clover honey

1 large lemon

Dissolve honey in the water and stir well. Beat the egg whites and stir this in also. Simmer, stirring all the time. Let it cool until barely lukewarm and add the yeast mixed with a little water and sugar. Next add peel and juice of the lemon. Allow to ferment in a jar with an airlock. Siphon into bottles, seal and store. This was given to me as a "fast" recipe for mead, which can be drunk after one week.

RUM SORBET

225g (8oz) sugar

600ml (1 pint) water

juice of ½ lemon and its peeled rind

juice of 1 orange (strained)

juice of 1 lemon (strained)

1 glass rum

Put sugar, water, lemon rind and juice of ½ lemon into pan and heat gently so that sugar dissolves but does not burn. Boil for 10 minutes but do not stir. Strain this syrup and leave to go cold.

Measure 300ml (½ pint) of the syrup. Add the strained fruit juices and rum. Pour into a shallow porcelain container, cover with foil and freeze for 25 minutes. Turn into bowl and stir well, then leave in freezer compartment until required.

ROSEMARY SYRUP

A good handful of rosemary leaves

1.2l (2 pints) water

sugar

Cut up rosemary and pour boiling water onto it. Cover and leave near fire for 3 hours. Strain the liquor. To each pint (600ml) add 450g (1lb) sugar and boil until syrupy.

Mother's Hedgerow Jam was always a winner, made from rose hips, sloes, blackberries, wild strawberries. Her Wild Blackberry Pie she made by first cooking the blackberries (which are usually very "seedy") and straining the juice from them onto gently cooked apple, a union which resulted in splendid, fruity filling, without the crunchiness of seeds which can be excruciating when they wander under dental plates. However, she never made wine, classing it with "strong drink" which she would not touch, having signed the Temperance Pledge when she was sixteen.

At Rock, besides these old, handsome, timbered cottages, is the Church of St Peter and St Paul which has a very old Parish Chest and magnificent Norman arches within and without. Ralph de Tosny III who was present at the Battle of Hastings gave Rock Church and part of Wyre Forest to a group of Normandy Monks in the 12th Century. Grooved marks on the external walls were probably made in 1405 "by the sharpening of weapons" when the Welsh under Owen Glendower faced the English at Abberley Hill.

95

HEDGEROW WINE

This recipe from Wyre Forest has an ecclesiastical source and must surely have been made since wild blackberries bloomed in early Autumn and the fruits of the forest were noticed by hungry natives.

4.5l (1 gallon) wild blackberries	1kg (2lb) sloes
4.5l (1 gallon) boiling water	225g (8oz) sugar
15g (½oz) yeast	1 slice of toast

Wash the fruit, then pour the boiling water over it. Leave for one week. Each day mash the fruit with a wooden spoon. Strain and squeeze all the liquid from the fruit. Strain through muslin and add the sugar, stirring until quite dissolved. The yeast should then be spread upon the toast and floated on the wine which can then be placed in a warm area to ferment. After a week it can be skimmed and bottled.

◆

Instead of the cold tea served to most agricultural workers at harvest time, home-brewed herb beer was provided for forest workers as it was found that the men worked better off this. I was interested to hear about the old custom of sealing a bargain with a mug of ale at the Mug House, Bewdley.

When we four children were growing up, with unfailing regularity father made pickled walnuts, home-made wines and herb beer. In those days wines were usually made in a 18l (4 gallon) cask. Ours, passed down in the family, was well seasoned. Bottles had to be scrupulously clean, although he used mainly screw-top jars, and his rules were:

- Use new corks.
- Bottle wine in dry weather.
- When bottling, do not shake the cask.
- Fruit and vegetables should be perfect, scrupulously clean and gathered in dry weather.
- Storing temperature 55 F./13°C.
- The bung hole of the cask should be left open until all fermentation has ceased; put simply that is when the hissing noise can no longer be heard. A bowl was kept under the cask to catch the scum. While fermentation is going on the cask should be in a warm place. Ours was kept near the hearth stone, and later the liquid was put into the stone jars.

We were allowed to drink the herb beer and it tasted good, being very cooling in hot weather. When I was four I watched my father opening a jar. Suddenly the screw top took off like a genie and herb beer splattered the ceiling. I was very impressed.

HERB BEER

"In 9l (2 gallons) of water a few handfuls of clean, fresh, young plants of stinging nettles and a few handfuls of dandelions should be boiled for half an hour with 50g (2oz) of bruised root ginger. After straining, pieces of toasted bread, on which have been spread a small quantity of brewer's yeast, should be placed in the liquor. When fermentation is over, 25g (1oz) cream of tartar to be added and after further straining the beer can be bottled and corked."

If using bottles, as most people do nowadays, they must be scrupulously clean and dry. Pour the liquor into them but do not cork until fermentation has ceased. One aunt used tight, little rolls of linen shaped like corks, which could be pressed lightly into the bottles. If corked tightly too soon, the bottles could explode. Cork and seal according to the directions in the recipe. When the wines have matured and all sediment is at the bottom, pour off carefully without disturbing the sediment. Strain and put into fresh bottles.

◆

DAMSON GIN

A simple, old damson gin recipe was as follows:

1.5kg (3lb) damsons   1.5kg (3lb) sugar
1 large bottle of gin

Place the well-washed damsons in a large jar with a screw top. Put sugar over the top and pour the gin over. Screw down and keep until Christmas. Pour off the liquid and bottle.

I believe gin lovers may have adapted this recipe, using sloes instead of damsons, since most of the recipes I received which used sloes were for making into jelly. This one is particularly good with cold pork.

◆

ELDERFLOWER WINE

4.5l (1 gallon) elderflowers
(remove as much stalks as possible with fork)
1.5kg (3lb) sugar
1 lemon
1 sachet (Hock) type wine maker's yeast
approx 4.5l (1 gallon) water

Place elderflowers, diced lemon (peel and all) and pour on the water at boiling point. Cover with a cloth or tea towel to keep out insects and leave for 5-6 days, stirring once or twice in that time. It will probably start to ferment a bit naturally. At about 6 days, strain and bring the liquid to the boil and allow to cool, still keeping covered. When cool, stir in yeast and sugar, place in a Winchester with air locks and ferment, topping up with sugar occasionally, adding more if a sweet wine is liked. When fermentation is finished, the wine can be racked off into another Winchester and kept for 6 months before bottling, keeping well corked. This produces a better wine than immediate bottling. Should be served chilled. Good with cold lamb or chicken.

Sometimes these flower wines start to fizz a little at about a year after the flowers were picked. If this is excessive it means that fermentation was not complete and the corks will blow out; if only slight, one gets an agreeable slightly sparkling wine

ELDERBERRY WINE I

9l (8 quarts) elderberries
2.75kg (6lb) Demerara sugar
100g (4oz) ground ginger
piece of toast

9l (8 quarts) water
15g (½oz) Allspice
2 tablespoons yeast

The berries should be black and ripe (watch the starlings; they know). Strip from stalks and measure. Place in pan and pour water over them, stirring and pressing well. Each day for five days continue to stir and press, then press out as much juice as possible through a hair sieve. Measure the juice, putting 9l (8 quarts) into a preserving pan with the sugar and spices. Gently boil all for ¼ hour then strain into a porcelain dish, floating on the toast spread with yeast. Cover with a cloth and leave for four days. After skimming, place in a cask and make sure the bung is left loose until hissing ceases. Only then should it be bunged tightly. Leave four months before bottling.

PLUM WINE

1.75kg (4lb) plums
1.5kg (3lb) granulated sugar
a stick of cinnamon

4.5l (1 gallon) water
25g (1oz) root ginger
15 cloves

"Remove stalks from plums and wipe with a cloth. Place in an earthenware bowl or ceramic dish along with the ginger, cinnamon and cloves. Cover with 4.5l (1 gallon) of boiling water and leave for a fortnight, stirring night and morning. Then add the sugar, stirring well until all has completely dissolved. Strain into a cask and in six months' time the plum wine will be ready to bottle."

ELDERBERRY WINE II

1.5kg (3lb)sugar   3.75kg (8lb) ripe elderberries
50g (2oz) yeast
15g (½oz) mixed spice and ginger to every 4.5l (gallon)

Boil the berries for ½ hour then strain. Add 1.5kg (3lb) sugar, mixed spice and ginger to every 4.5l (gallon). The mixed spice should be contained in a muslin bag. Remove scum as it rises. When cold, ferment with yeast spread on toast. After 3 days add 450g (1lb) seedless raisins (muscatel type). Leave for 6 weeks, then strain and bottle.

◆

ELDERBERRY WINE III

Collect about half a pail of elderberries on a fine, sunny day, wash and cover with water in a preserving pan. Boil until liquid is dark red; avoid crushing the berries. Measure off, and to every 1.2l (quart) of liquid add 450g (1lb) sugar. Boil again and strain again. When cool, put a slice of toasted bread spread with 50g (2oz) yeast to float on top of the liquid and allow it to stay for 3 days. Skim and strain. Put in bottles without corks for 5 weeks. Just before corking add 1 tablespoon of whisky to each bottle.

BEETROOT WINE

1.75kg (4lb)beetroot

3 lemons

40g (1½oz) yeast

225g (½lb)sultanas

1.5kg (3lb)sugar

Wash beetroot well, remove tops, cut into slices and place in a pan with 4.5l (1 gallon) of water. Boil until the beetroot is pale. Strain the liquid off and place in a large jar with the sultanas and sliced lemons with pips removed. Cool. Add the sugar and yeast. Leave for 2 weeks, stirring each day with a wooden spoon. Strain again and cover with muslin. Leave until fermentation has finished. Bottle and leave for 2 months. The lady who gave this recipe said, "It is better than port."

This beautiful three-arch bridge spanning the River Severn was built by Thomas Telford with stone taken from the estate of Lord Valencia at Arley and the quarry at Highley. John Simpson, stonemason, of Shrewsbury, oversaw the building which cost £11,000. 500 years ago this waterway was busier than any in Britain and Bewdley was one of the busiest inland ports.

MUSCATEL RAISIN WINE

Although some Health Food shops sell them before Christmas, even if you could track them down, to buy 3.75kg (8lb) of muscatel raisins would these days involve much expense. Ordinary raisins can be used but the real thing must have been delicious. Here is the recipe as given. The end product, I am told, was a great favourite of the village parson many years ago.

3.75g (8lb) muscatel raisins   9l (2 gallons) water
150ml (¼ pint) brandy

Remove the branch stems and place the muscatels in a container, adding the water. Press down and cover with a linen cloth. For four weeks every day the raisins should be stirred and pressed well. Strain off the rich liquor, pressing hard on the raisins to get every drop. Pour this liquor into a cask and bung lightly. When there is no further hissing sound, bung tightly and leave for a year. Strain the wine through muslin into another cask. Add the brandy and leave for a further two years before bottling.

I have read church magazines from the 1870s which contained recipes. I wonder if the vicar included an annual reminder on muscatel raisin wine. Three years was otherwise a long time to wait.

◆

POTATO WINE

When potatoes were being lifted the tiny ones were heaped together to go into potato wine.

2.25l (½ gallon) potatoes   1.5kg (3lb) Demerara sugar
4.5l (1 gallon) water   the grated rind of 3 oranges
the juice of 4 lemons

Scrub the potatoes (any large ones may be halved). Boil them in the water for 15 minutes. Slice the lemons and place in a big earthenware dish. Add the orange rind and the sugar. Strain the liquor from the potatoes and pour this over the lemons etc. Boil gently for 30 minutes then strain through muslin. When it is cold, bottle and cork securely. It can be drunk within two weeks but it improves with keeping.

◆

DANDELION WINE

2.25l (4 pints) dandelion flowers (no stalks)
4.5l (8 pints) boiling water   1.5kg (3lb)sugar
1 teaspoon citric acid   2 teaspoons wine yeast compound

Place the rinsed and drained flower heads in a bucket. Pour on 4.5l (1 gallon) of boiling water and leave for five days. Strain this liquor onto the sugar and ensure the latter dissolves. Stir in the citric acid. Sprinkle on 2 teaspoons of the yeast compound.

This wine is cold fermented. Leave at room temperature. Fermentation takes longer. "Rack off" when clear.

Callow Hill. A lovely area of Wyre Forest, one of the most important broad-leaved woodlands and National Nature Reserves in the country, consisting of over 6,000 acres, stretching westwards from Cleobury Mortimer well into Shropshire. Forest hamlets like Rock, Pensax, Bliss Gate and Far Forest (made famous by author Francis Brett Young) are formed where traditional forest crafts developed over the centuries. A herd of 300-400 fallow deer roam the forest. These are carefully counted and culled annually to keep deer stock healthy.

107

RASPBERRY GIN

A late recipe from a Midlands couple, Mr and Mrs Ray Williams, who regard this as a "must". "Must", in wine-making is the fruit pulp.

1kg (2lb) ripe raspberries   600ml (1 pint) gin
1.2l (2 pints) water   450g (1lb) sugar

Place the cleaned fruit and the gin in a large jar. It should be allowed to stand in a warm spot for five days, the jar taken up and shaken whenever you remember. In a large saucepan bring the water to the boil. Add sugar and boil gently for 15 minutes. Allow to cool and add to the fruit. Screw the jar up tightly and store in a dark, dry cupboard for three months, occasionally turning the jar. Strain through a fine jelly bag and bottle. Ready for Christmas. Do not discard the fruit pulp as it is excellent with Queen Victoria's Shortbread, the recipe for which is on another page.

These recipes, passed on as tried and tested over many years, can be easily adapted to modern wine-making and equipment. Setting us in the right direction were the "fruity passions" of Margaret Vaughan and Mary Hardiman-Jones. They too stress the importance of sterilising equipment and keeping containers covered.

◆

WINE MAKING EQUIPMENT

A 9l (2 gallon) white plastic fermentation bucket with a plastic lid.

An enamel or stainless steel pan (not brass or copper).

A long-handled wooden spoon and bottle brush.

A large nylon sieve or straining bag.

Nowadays, for the all-important job of sterilising, Campden tablets dissolved in water to form a sulphite solution, are obtainable. Our big, glazed, earthenware bowl, nearly 100 years old, is still considered excellent, and if, like grandfather, you have real crystal spring water at your disposal, that is indeed an ace in the pack. Certainly you must avoid a coloured plastic bucket and wine should not stand for long in a metal container.

Instead of casks we now talk of a demi john or fermentation jar with rubber bung with a hole in it to fit in the top of the jar. A glass or plastic airlock fits into this bung.

For siphoning or "racking off", a second demi john or empty cider jar is needed and a solid rubber bung to seal. A 1.2m (4 ft.) long transparent tube is used to siphon the wine from one demi john to the other.

The wine can be stored in demi johns or earthenware jars but most people prefer to bottle it: dark green bottles for red wine; pale green or brown for white. Six bottles hold 4.5l (1 gallon) a packet of corks, labels and a simple corking tool can be had, like the rest of this equipment, from the Home Wine-Making departments of Boots. When I recall what grandad, in his simplicity achieved, I cannot think that sophisticated extras like heated winter jackets for your fermentation jar are really necessary. However, the yeasts cultivated especially for today's wine-making are very good and it is worth substituting these for old-fashioned brewers' yeast. These are sold in sachets which should be rehydrated with a little warm water five minutes before using.

Let Margaret Vaughan have the last word: "The most common cause of home-made wines going wrong is contamination from one of many kinds of bacteria. The answer is first to wash and then sterilise all your equipment properly."

♦

HONEY

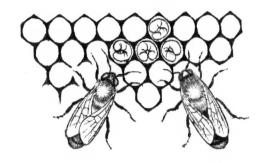

Honey Cookery

The use of honey in Wyre Forest recipes was more marked than in other regions visited – again not surprising as with much blossom from a wide variety of plants, Worcestershire honey must for centuries past have been readily available. Pliny the Elder wrote, when he visited Britain, "These islanders consume great quantities of honey brew" – meaning mead. He believed it was good for health and long life and reports that he met 124 bee keepers all of whom were over 100 years old. A 17th century farmer's wife in her diary regrets that in getting the honey they had to kill the bees the only way they knew: " . . . dig a hole in the ground for each skeppe where we put a sulfur paper, set alight and put the skeppe of bees on the topp . . . we do want the honey, using a gret lot in the hous." Their favourite was "Honey cake and rollies", but in Wyre area it was used extensively in many culinary pursuits. "Telling" the bees is an old custom in a number of counties especially when the head of the house dies. This is so the bees will not forsake them.

◆

SWEET PICKLE

6 cloves   1 cup vinegar

2 cups Worcestershire clover   2 pinches cinnamon

1.5kg (3lb) washed, quartered apples

honey

Mix honey, vinegar, cinnamon and cloves together and boil. Cook ¼ of the apples in this syrup. When cooked, carefully remove apples and cook the rest of the apples in the same way. Remove cloves from syrup. Store the apples in sterilised jars, pouring the syrup equally divided over them. Seal and label. This is a useful way to use windfall apples which in some years were so plentiful in Worcestershire and Oxfordshire that passers by were invited to take whatever they wanted. The golden rule is to use delicately flavoured honeys with light ingredients and the stronger honeys with strong-flavoured ingredients.

Ribbesford Avenue is photographed in 1916. the Manor of Ribbesford being given to the Herberts by Charles I. George Herbert, the poet, belonged to this family and Sir Henry Herbert was Master of the King's Revels. The present domed and turreted house stands on the original site. Alongside the walled garden of the Manor House is the Norman Church of St Leonard.

HONEY PUDDING

50g (2oz) butter   1 egg
8 tablespoons honey   150ml (¼ pint) milk
100g (4oz) seedless raisins   175g (6oz) S.R.flour

Blend together the butter and honey. Beat in the egg and milk.
Stir in the sieved flour and raisins. Turn into a greased pudding
basin large enough for mixture to rise in, placing a greased disc
of greaseproof paper at bottom of basin. Can be cooked in
pressure cooker or steamed for 2-3 hours in traditional way.
Very good with custard.

◆

CURRANT PUDDING

350g (12oz) S.R. flour   100g (4oz) shredded suet
75g (3oz) caster sugar   175g (6oz) currants
milk to mix   1 tablespoon honey

Sift together flour and a pinch of sea salt. Stir in suet, sugar,
honey and currants. Mix with sufficient milk to form a soft but
not sticky dough. Put into a large basin and cover with a double
layer of greaseproof paper, loosely placed. Steam for 2-2½
hours. Serve with custard.

The donor of this recipe says it is excellent cooked in the
microwave oven.

SYRUP SPONGE

225g (8oz) sifted S.R. flour

½ teaspoon bicarbonate of soda

3 tablespoons golden syrup

150ml scant(¼ pint) boiling water

175g (6oz) sugar

1 egg

150g (5oz) butter

Beat the egg well and place in mixing bowl. Add flour and bicarbonate of soda. Next stir in sugar and syrup, then add butter and pour over it the boiling water. Mix all ingredients well and when smooth, pour into baking tin and bake at 170°C for about an hour. More melted syrup over the pudding when serving makes it a children's delight, but make sure they clean their teeth well after this indulgent old favourite. Honey can be used instead.

◆

CREAMED RICE PUDDING

1.2l (2 pints) milk

75g (3oz) brown sugar

3 tablespoons honey

100g (4oz) ground rice

2 tablespoons orange flower water

75g (3oz) chopped almonds

Boil milk. Mix ground rice to a paste with 150ml (¼ pint) of milk and pour this into the milk, stirring well to avoid lumps and cook over low heat until it thickens. Add sugar then orange flower water, still stirring well all the time. Pour into a dish and cool. Gently heat the honey until it melts, with 4 tablespoons of water. Pour over pudding and scatter nuts. The honey sauce may be added to the usual baked rice pudding. Either way, children love it.

PICKLED RED CABBAGE

1 red cabbage sliced up   50g (2oz) butter
1 grated cooking apple   3 tablespoons honey
3 tablespoons cider vinegar or malt vinegar

Heat butter in a cast iron enamelled pan. Add honey and stir well. Put in shredded cabbage, working into butter and honey. Add 12 grinds of peppercorn, the grated apple, vinegar and a small quantity of any good stock. Cook for ¾ hour, adding more liquid as necessary.

◆

ABBERLEY HONEY ROAST

1 gammon joint   225g (8oz) clover honey
2 teaspoons powdered mustard   150ml (1 gill) cider
cloves

Soak the joint for 24 hours, changing the water at least 6 times to remove salt from ham. Wrap joint in foil like a parcel, as secure and airtight as possible. Cook in pre-heated oven at 180°C, allowing 15 minutes per 450g (lb) plus 15 minutes. 20 minutes before end of cooking time, remove foil, cut fat on ham in diamond shapes with a sharp knife and place a clove in the centre of each. Mix the mustard with the honey, spreading this over the ham. Return to the oven, baste frequently with the juices and the cider. The ham will turn a golden brown and when cold, further decoration with cherries and orange segments makes it look even more mouth-watering when brought to the table.

SAYERS TOMATO CHUTNEY

1.75g (4lb) tomatoes   450g (1lb) apples

1 kg (2lb) sultanas   1 large onion

450g (1lb) clover honey   juice of 2 lemons

½ cup malt vinegar   ½ teaspoon crushed cloves

1 teaspoon salt

225g (½lb) dates washed and pre-soaked in water

Pour boiling water over the tomatoes to split the skins. Peel and cut up tomatoes, apples, onion, and stir in other ingredients. Boil for 2 hours in a well-sealed kitchen, otherwise the scent of vinegar permeates the house. Pack into sterilised bottles, seal and label.

Honey can be used to glaze game, chicken and lamb cutlets, and to take the place of sugar in desserts and puddings. Indeed, stewed fruits are vastly improved by honey rather than by adding sugar. Grilled, honeyed grapefruit, uncooked strawberries, blackberries or raspberries, dribbled with honey, all make quick, easy and beneficial sweets.

HONEY NUT TOFFEE

225g (½lb) honey   100g (¼lb) chopped nuts

Boil the honey in a strong saucepan for 12 minutes. Have a greased tin handy covered with the chopped nuts. Pour honey onto the nuts. When cold, it can be broken into lumps and wrapped as individual pieces, using screws of greaseproof paper.

STUFFED DATES

These dates are stuffed with the honey nut toffee. Use good quality boxed dates. Remove stones from dates. Fill the holes with the honey nut toffee.

◆

TRUFFLES

50g (2oz) caster sugar	50g (2oz) unsalted butter
100g (4oz) ground almonds	2 teaspoons cocoa
finely grated breadcrumbs from crusts	lemon juice
grated plain chocolate to coat	honey

Cream butter and sugar until light and fluffy, add cocoa powder, almonds and enough fine crumbs to make a workable paste. Add small quantity of lemon juice but be careful not to make the paste soggy. Knead well and roll into long sausage. Cut into 1cm (½ inch) pieces and further roll into balls. Toss into the honey and then roll into the grated chocolate so that every truffle is generously coated.

◆

John Tolley, coal merchant, photographed with his horse and heavy, plank-sided, Worcestershire cart in Dog Lane, Bewdley, about 1902, a time when great flocks of geese were driven for rearing to the fattening farms because Michaelmas Goose was a favourite dish. Large white cross Tamworth pigs were reared and stallions travelled between farms or staging posts (inns), showing their pedigree stud cards The servicing fee was 1 guinea and 2/6d for the groom who walked beside the stallion. With so many horses necessary for carting, the blacksmiths were very busy shoeing them at the smithies, but it is good to read that "the horses had a holiday in the summer".

FRUIT. VEGETABLES.

Fruit and Vegetable Dishes

As we sped towards Bewdley, passing mellow, red-brick barns cloaked in early-morning mist, we caught sight of the plume of white smoke from a Severn Valley Railway engine, its gleaming coppernob reflecting the sun's rays and travelling the 16 miles between Bridgnorth and Kidderminster. We walked miles through this lovely Georgian town with its incomparable river setting, meeting shoppers and tradespeople, like Michael Pulsford of Forget-Me-Not Woodcraft, who likes a juicy steak. Interesting visits to the Museum and Brass Rubbing Centre over, we made for the three-arched span Telford Bridge, past the George and the many magpie houses, to the Cock and Pye. Feeling ravenously hungry in the sharp, early spring air and wondering what they ate at the Old Pals' Shelter, by evening we were tucking into excellent, piping hot fish and chips at the corner of Coles Quay.

One would expect an area well blessed by nature for the production of splendid fruit and vegetables to exploit these, as Wyre Forest district does. Shops and markets in Kidderminster, Bewdley and Stourport display a great range. Years ago, cherries, plums, damsons, pears and apples were all carefully packed in fern from the forest prior to sending off to London and Manchester.

---◆---

BLACKBERRY CURD

This was a completely new and delicious sweetmeat to us, but not really surprising as blackberries must have been widely and readily available in Wyre Forest for centuries. This recipe makes 2.7kg (6lb)

1kg (2lb) blackberries	350g (¾lb) apples
225g (8oz) butter	6 eggs
juice of 2 lemons	1.25kg (2½lb) lump sugar
water to cover	

Simmer the peeled and cored apples and the blackberries in sufficient water to cover, until the fruit is soft. Pour through a sieve into a double boiler. Add the lemon juice, cut up butter and sugar. When all has dissolved add the strained, well-beaten eggs and cook until mixture thickens, stirring all the time. When the mixture coats the back of the wooden spoon, it is ready. Pour into warm, sterilised jars and seal, but do not expect to store it as long as jam.

◆

SLOE JELLY

2.75kg (6lb) sloes washed and pricked
1.75l (3pints) water

Simmer until tender then mash well. Strain through a jelly bag overnight. Measure the juice and bring to the boil, stirring in 450g (1lb) of sugar for each 600ml (1 pint) of juice. Boil until setting point reached and pour into clean jars.

The Tontine, overlooking the Canal Basin at Stourport-on-Severn, offers traditional draught beers and food, but in 1788 it was owned by the Canal Company, the houses on each side of the original inn being used by hop merchants. When refused at Bewdley, James Brindley brought the canal to Stourport, following the Stour Valley and joining the Severn at this point. Stourport, with its quay and warehouses, replaced Bewdley as an inland port, and although its commercial traffic has gone, it retains its colourful history. Canal bridges are scored and worn by the ropes of the horses that used to pull the narrow boats.

BLACKCURRANT FOOL

450g (1lb) blackcurrants

100g (4oz) caster sugar

450ml (¾ pint) full cream milk

150ml (¼ pint) cream

2 tablespoons custard powder

Cook the blackcurrants with 75g (3oz) sugar until soft, simmering gently. Put the milk on to heat, taking sufficient to mix the custard powder and the remaining sugar to a smooth cream. Add to the milk when nearly boiling and stir for a few minutes. Strain the blackcurrants, saving the juice and sieving the fruit. Stir the fruit puree into the custard when the latter is quite cold, adding the cream and some of the blackcurrant juice to achieve a nice consistency. Put into individual glasses and serve chilled with thick cream or yoghurt.

---◆---

GOOSEBERRY FOOL

450g (1lb) gooseberries, washed, topped, tailed

300ml (½ pint) double cream

100g (4oz) sugar

Simmer the fruit and sugar with a little water in a stainless steel pan. Put the fruit mixture in a blender and turn it into a puree. Whisk the double cream until stiff then fold in the cold puree. Looks nicest in individual glasses with a star of cream piped on after chilling for about an hour.

GOOSEBERRY AND ELDERFLOWER FOOL

My grandmother was a great believer in swishing creamy elderflowers through gooseberry jam in the cooking to improve flavour so she would have liked this recipe.

450g (1lb) gooseberries   100g (4oz) sugar
3 heads elderflower   150ml (¼ pint) double cream

Clean the gooseberries but do not top or tail. Cook in the sugar over low heat until fruit is soft and mushy. Remove pan from heat and add the elderflowers, stirring gently. Leave for 5 minutes then discard the flowers. Liquidise the fruit and allow to go cold. Whisk the cream and fold into the gooseberry puree. Leave at the bottom of the fridge until ready to serve.

ORANGE MEDLEY

1 tablespoon natural yoghourt   1 free range egg
300ml (½ pint) freshly squeezed orange juice   1 banana

Blend all to a puree. Chill and serve.

BLACKCURRANT JAM

1.75kg (4lb) blackcurrants
2.25kg (5lb) preserving sugar

1 tablespoon lemon juice
5 450g (1lb) jars of water

Cook fruit in the water for about 30 minutes (in some seasons the skins of blackcurrants are tough). Add the sugar and lemon juice and boil until a set is achieved. Pot and seal.

◆

DAMSON JAM

2 kg (4½lb) damsons
2.25kg (5lb) preserving sugar

900ml (1½ pints) water

Wash damsons, removing stalks and leaves. Slit the damsons with a sharp knife. Put the fruit and water into a large, buttered jam pan and simmer over gentle heat for 25 minutes until fruit is tender. Pour in the warmed sugar gradually until all of it is completely dissolved. Bring to boil. Boil rapidly for 10 minutes at least, skimming off the stones as they rise. Test for set, then, allowing to cool a little, use a Pyrex jug to decant the jam into warm clean jars. The waxed discs can be moistened with brandy.

◆

The Pack Horse inn, near Lax Lane Corner, Bewdley, today serves exotic dishes: roast of lamb with herbs and apricots; grilled fresh sardines; shark steak; smoked mackerel; syrup pancakes, but this historic hostelry was once the point at which the pack horse trains assembled and loaded up. The long strings of mules carried "Kidderminster stuffs", leather, horn and ironware. The packmen in those days fed on deer, hare, wild fowl, rabbits and oatmeal gruel laced with brandy to brave the weather. Lax Lane runs the length of Snuff Mill Brook which once led to an ancient ford long before the first bridge was built in 1447.

GREENGAGE JAM

1.5kg (3lb) greengages   300ml (½ pint) water

1.5kg (3lb) preserving sugar

Wash fruit, remove stalks and place in preserving pan with
water. Simmer for 20 minutes. Warm sugar and gradually add
to pan. Stir over low heat until dissolved then boil rapidly for
15 minutes, removing stones as they bubble up. When almost
ready, add 50g (2oz) chopped, blanched almonds.

◆

BAYTON RASPBERRY JAM

This Wyre Forest recipe for raspberry jam makes the best
possible tasting, but "do not make up more than 1.75kg (4lb) of
raspberries at a time."

1.75kg (4lb) raspberries   2.25kg (5lb) preserving

                                           sugar

Put raspberries in a heavy preserving pan over gentle heat.
Mash with a wooden spoon until juices run. The warmed sugar
should then be added and, once dissolved, brought quickly to
the boil, allowing three minutes and no more. Pour into jars and
seal. Used in a winter pudding with a light sponge, it brings
summer into the room and is the best filling for Victoria Sponge
cake or with Queen Victoria's Shortbread, which can be found
amongst "Bread, Cakes etc".

TANGERINE MARMALADE

1 grapefruit

1.5kg (3lb) tangerines

2.25kg (5lb) preserving sugar

1 large lemon

2.75l (5 pints) water

1 teaspoon tartaric acid

Scrub the fruit, removing peel from tangerines, and cut this into very fine shreds. Tie in a muslin bag and put into pan with fruit and water. Stir in the tartaric acid. Simmer gently for 2 hours then take out the muslin bag. Strain the fruit pulp through a scalded cloth or a jelly bag overnight. Next day measure the juice. In a clean preserving pan place juice and sugar and stir until dissolved. Boil rapidly until setting point is reached.

◆

ROWAN JELLY

1.5kg (3lb) rowan berries   450g (1lb) apples

preserving sugar

Remove stalks and wash berries. Wash apples and chop. Put fruit in a preserving pan with sufficient water to cover and simmer for 50 minutes. Strain through a jelly bag and measure the yield. Return to pan and allow 450g (1lb) of sugar to each 600ml (pint) of fruit juice. Stir until sugar has dissolved and boil rapidly until setting point is reached. Test, then pour into warmed jars.

Excellent with lamb or venison. It is important to use genuine preserving sugar to get a jewel-clear appearance in the jelly. A sweeter jelly can be made by using equal quantities of rowans and apples and by increasing the sugar.

MARROW PROVENCALE

1 medium-sized marrow

2 large peeled, finely chopped onions

1 peeled, crushed clove of garlic

2 teaspoons Herbes de Provence

4 large, skinned, chopped tomatoes

1 tablespoon corn oil

salt and pepper

Peel and cut the marrow into cubes, discarding the seeds. Cook onions and garlic for five minutes in the oil. Add the cubed marrow and fry for a further five minutes. Stir in all the other ingredients and simmer for 30 minutes, stirring occasionally until all the vegetables are tender. Serve very hot.

STUFFED MARROW

1 vegetable marrow medium in size
1 chopped, peeled onion
100g (4oz) chopped, washed mushrooms
25g (1oz) Danish butter
5 skinned, well chopped, ripe tomatoes
good pinch of Herbes de Provence
175g (6oz) grated Lancashire cheese
4 tablespoonfuls fine breadcrumbs
a sprinkle of salt and a dash of pepper

Wash and halve the marrow, lengthwise, peel it and remove seeds. Cook the onion in the butter, add mushrooms and cook for one minute more. Stir the mixture of onions and mushrooms into the white sauce. Add herbs, tomatoes, seasoning, breadcrumbs and half of the grated cheese. Fill the marrow halves with this mixture and top with the remaining cheese. Wrap each half in foil and bake at 180°C for 1½ hours.

◆

ASPARAGUS PATE

275g (10oz) fresh asparagus   75g (3oz) melted butter
75g (3oz) cheese   1 tablespoon lemon juice
15g (½oz) gelatine dissolved in a little water
freshly ground salt and black peppercorns
2.5cm (1 inch) cucumber, chopped

Liquidise all the ingredients except the cucumber, then add the cucumber. Pour into a wetted mould to set then refrigerate. When turned out and brought to the table the pate can be decorated with more cucumber thinly sliced. Consume freshly made with wholemeal bread.

———————————— ◆ ————————————

BUTTERED ASPARAGUS

Asparagus is a special delicacy in the area close to Wyre Forest. The spears should be cut in season and are best eaten fresh from garden to pan. Around Midsummer Day you should no longer cut, allowing the plants to renew strength for next season.

Serve the spears cooked, with chopped tarragon and butter.

Another chef-recommended method of cooking is:

Trim dry ends from asparagus. Cook stalks upright in 7.5cm (3 inches) of boiling water with a hood of foil over the tips so that they cook gently in the steam. Cook for 15 minutes, then drain. Service with butter.

Charles Lamb, the essayist, believed that asparagus inspired gentle thoughts, so its use should spread beyond Wyre Forest.

ARTICHOKE MOUSSE WITH TOMATO SAUCE

150ml (¼ pint) Jerusalem artichoke puree

300ml (½ pint) double cream   1 whole egg

salt and ground white pepper   3 yolks of egg

Mix artichoke puree, cream and eggs (whole and yolk). Strain through a fine sieve and season to taste. Butter four 10cm (4 inch) ramekins and fill with mixture. Cover with tin foil and cook in a bain marie in oven on 200°C for 30-35 minutes, or until mixture is set to the touch. Serve hot with tomato sauce.

TOMATO SAUCE

8 soft tomatoes   50ml (2 fl.oz) water

1 dessertspoon tomato puree   175ml (6 fl.oz) double cream

2 shallots (or a small amount of chopped onion)

salt and ground white pepper

Place all ingredients in saucepan. Boil for 5 minutes, liquidise, strain and season.

TO FINISH

Unmould mousses on to plates. Pour hot sauce around, decorate with a small leaf (parsley, chervil e.g.)

This excellent photograph of Wribbenhall, across from Severnside, depicts a scene little changed over the centuries. Wribbenhall was a separate ancient village, having wharves and warehouses busy with Severn trows loading merchandise. William Beale, who came from Wribbenhall, is described in records as "barge-maker" and "ship-maker". In the 16th and 17th centuries goods sent from all over the Midlands by pack horse or carrier were then moved down river on the trows: wool, cloth, leather, nails, ironware, coal and stone.

AUBERGINE PATE - From Cleobury Mortimer

2 large aubergines

1 large onion

2 cloves garlic

3 tablespoons olive oil

1 tablespoon lemon juice

1 small onion

½ teaspoon salt

12 grinds of pepper

tomatoes, olives and parsley for garnish

Prick aubergines with a fork and bake in hot oven 200°C for 1 hour until soft and wrinkled. Peel and chop large onion and garlic and fry in olive oil until brown. Skin aubergines when cooked. Chop together aubergine flesh and all other ingredients except small raw onion and garnish. Chop small onion finely and mix into chopped aubergine. Decorate with slices of red tomato, black olives, green olives and chopped parsley. Chill before serving.

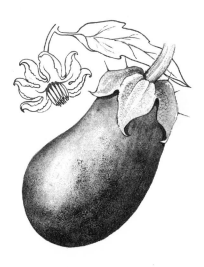

RECIPE INDEX

Page No.

Meat, Game and Fish

Soups and Savouries

Bread. Cakes. Puddings. Pies

Salads and Drinks

Honey

Fruit. Vegetables